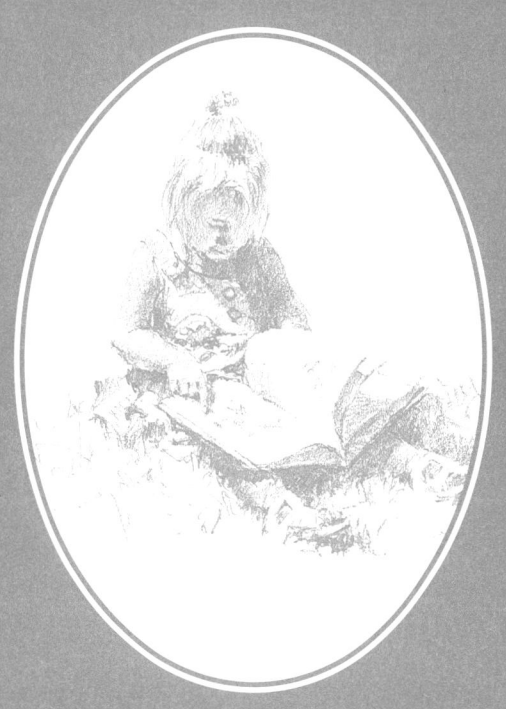

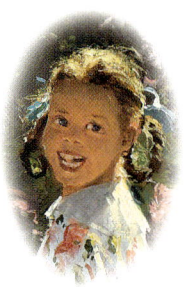

Copyright © 1998 Robert G. Hagan. All rights reserved.
No part of this book may be reproduced in any form or by any electronic or mechanical means including information storage and retrieval systems without permission in writing from the publisher, except by a reviewer, who may quote brief passages in a review.

Published by International Art Services Ltd.
Box HM 267, Hamilton, Bermuda. HMAX

Design by Primus, San Diego, USA
Color by Friendly Graphics Co., Hong Kong
Photography by Photodyne, San Diego, USA
Printed and Bound by Sun Fung Offset Binding Co. Ltd., Hong Kong

National Library of Canada
Cataloguing in Publication Data

Cherished Moments
Precious and Unforgettable Memories of Growing Up
/Robert Hagan

ISBN 0-9698515-1-0

Also by Robert Hagan
Images of Australia
Romantic Oil Painting Made Easy
Painting Cowboys and the Old West

Books published by International Art Services Ltd. are available at quantity discounts on the purchase of 10 or more copies of a single title for special markets or premium use. Special books or book excerpts can also be created to fit special needs. Please write to International Art Services Ltd., Box HM 267, Hamilton, Bermuda. HMAX

Preface and Acknowledgement

As an artist of passion I've never had much interest in painting anything that doesn't tell a story of some kind. The paintings I consider my best are generally the simplest. Simplest in execution and in story.

When I started on this book I knew I could paint from my heart and you know it doesn't really matter what neck of the woods we hail from. We all carry in our hearts similar desires, dreams and experiences. So somewhere in this book I hope we overlap!

Many people have been the subjects of my paintings in this book – some knowingly and others not knowing anything about it at all. If you happen to spot yourself in one of my paintings, then all I can say is thank you and God bless you for making my work so much easier!

To those who consciously gave their time to pose for me, I hope I have done you justice. You all wore your emotions on your sleeves and were a delight to work with. My thanks to Cortney and Shannon Stenger, Annette and Belinda Herd, Kelly and Lisa Anderson with their frisky little dog, Jock, Ylonda Perau, Wendy Cahill, Bridgette Pace, Amy and Leanne Rossington, Krystal Newell, Melissa Stenner, Heidi Rochester and close to home, Claire and Laura Hagan. A very special thanks to my daughter, Michelle, who apart from being my favourite model, has patiently put up with my artistic demands with a lot less complaints than she's entitled to.

A very special nod of appreciation to Janice Somera for allowing me to use some of her beautiful prose. Her work is inspirational to all.

I would also like to pay a special tribute to the many women in my life who have helped to navigate me back on course whenever, both physically and mentally, I've "gone walkabout" as they say in Australia. So thank you again Betty Stenger, Lynne Jordon, Carole McDowell, and, of course, my ever-forgiving mother Evelyn Hagan.

To those whose efforts in many various ways have helped to make this project possible thanks also to Alan Veitch, Len Torres, Bob Roeder, Randy Volheim, Bill Cahill, Bill Herd, Robert Gear, Rick Morris and my good mate, Don Stenger.

This book is dedicated with much love and admiration to my three wonderful children, Michelle, Joe and Graeme.

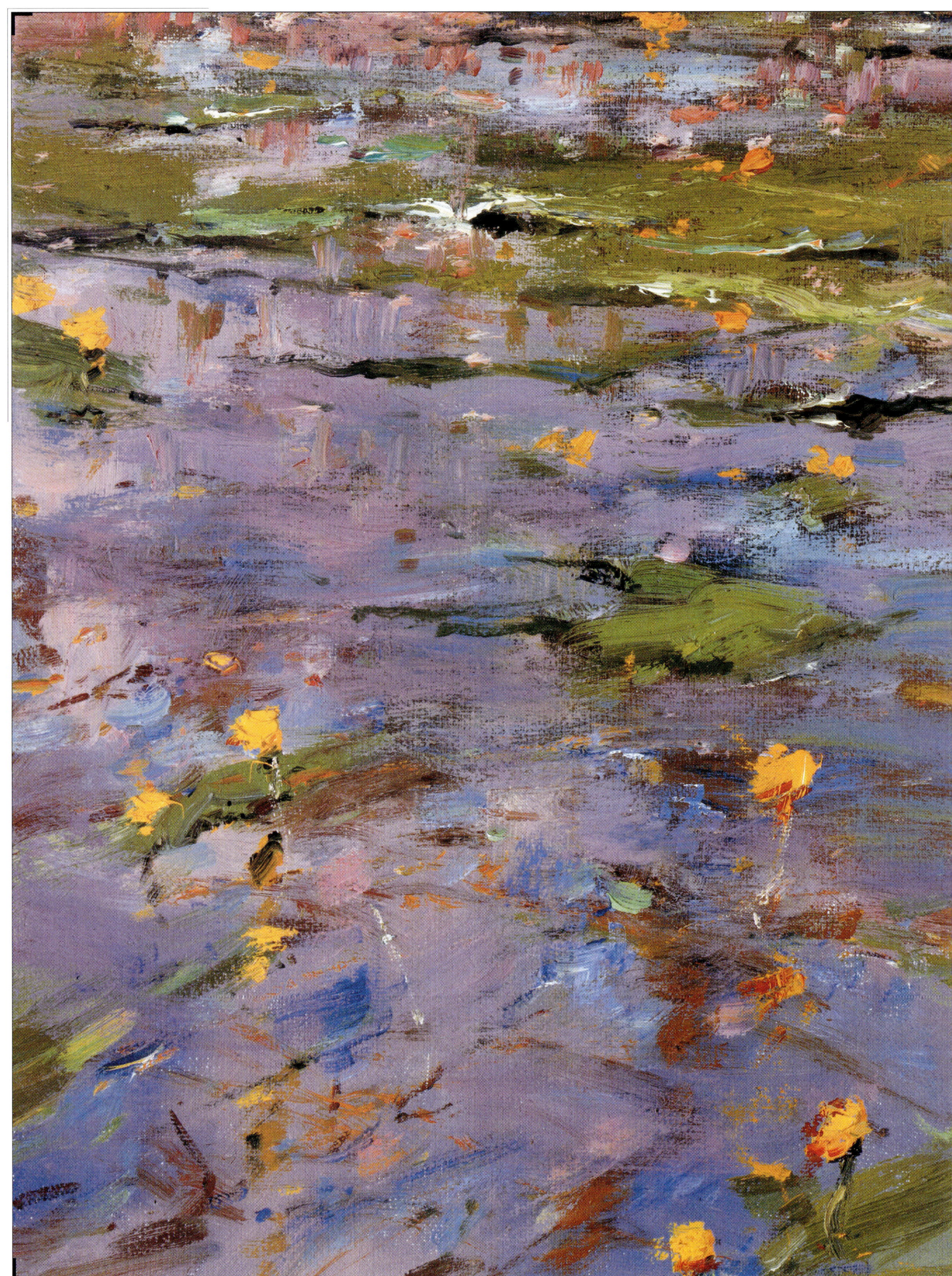

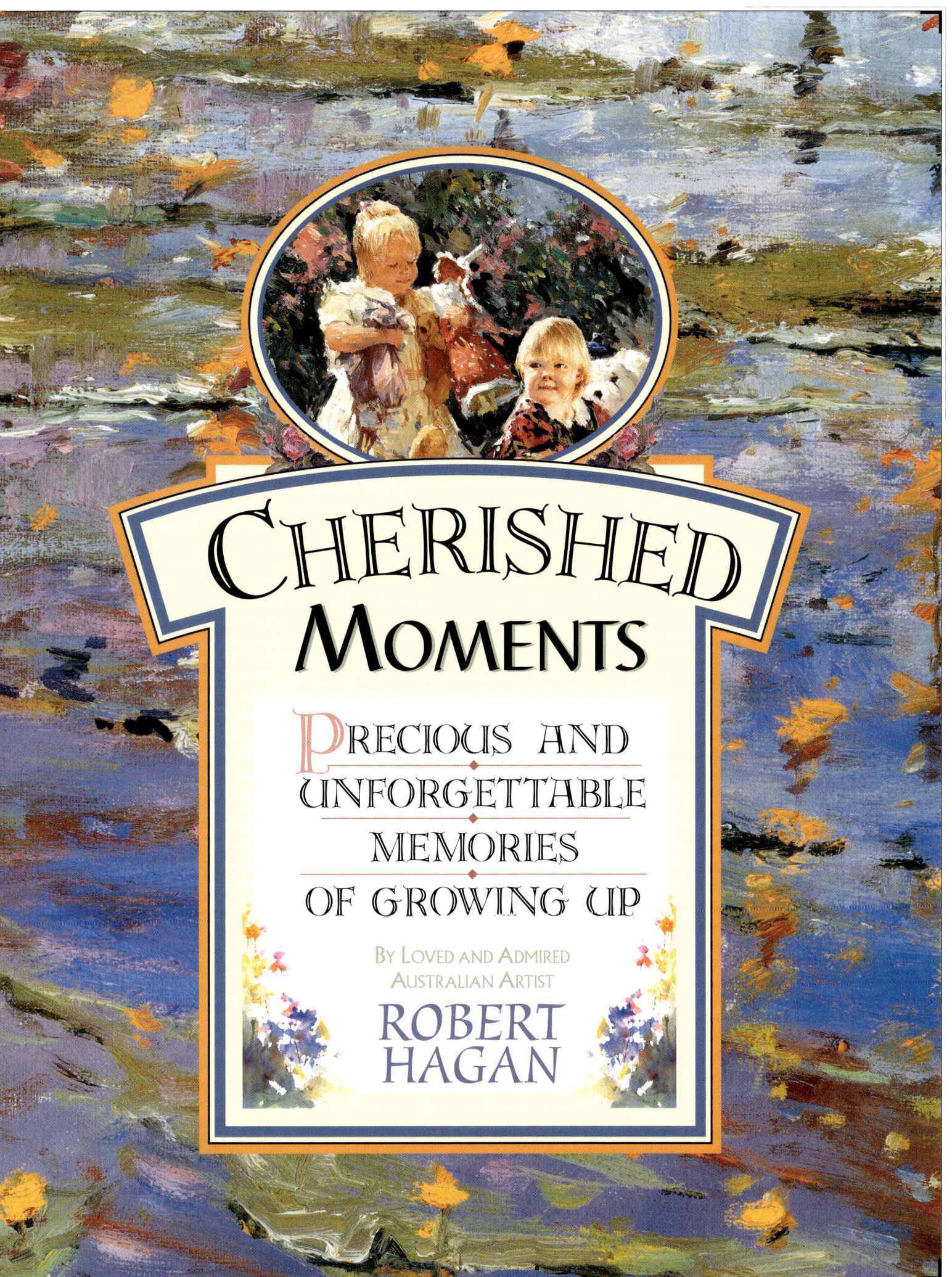

Cherished Moments

Precious and Unforgettable Memories of Growing Up

By Loved and Admired Australian Artist

Robert Hagan

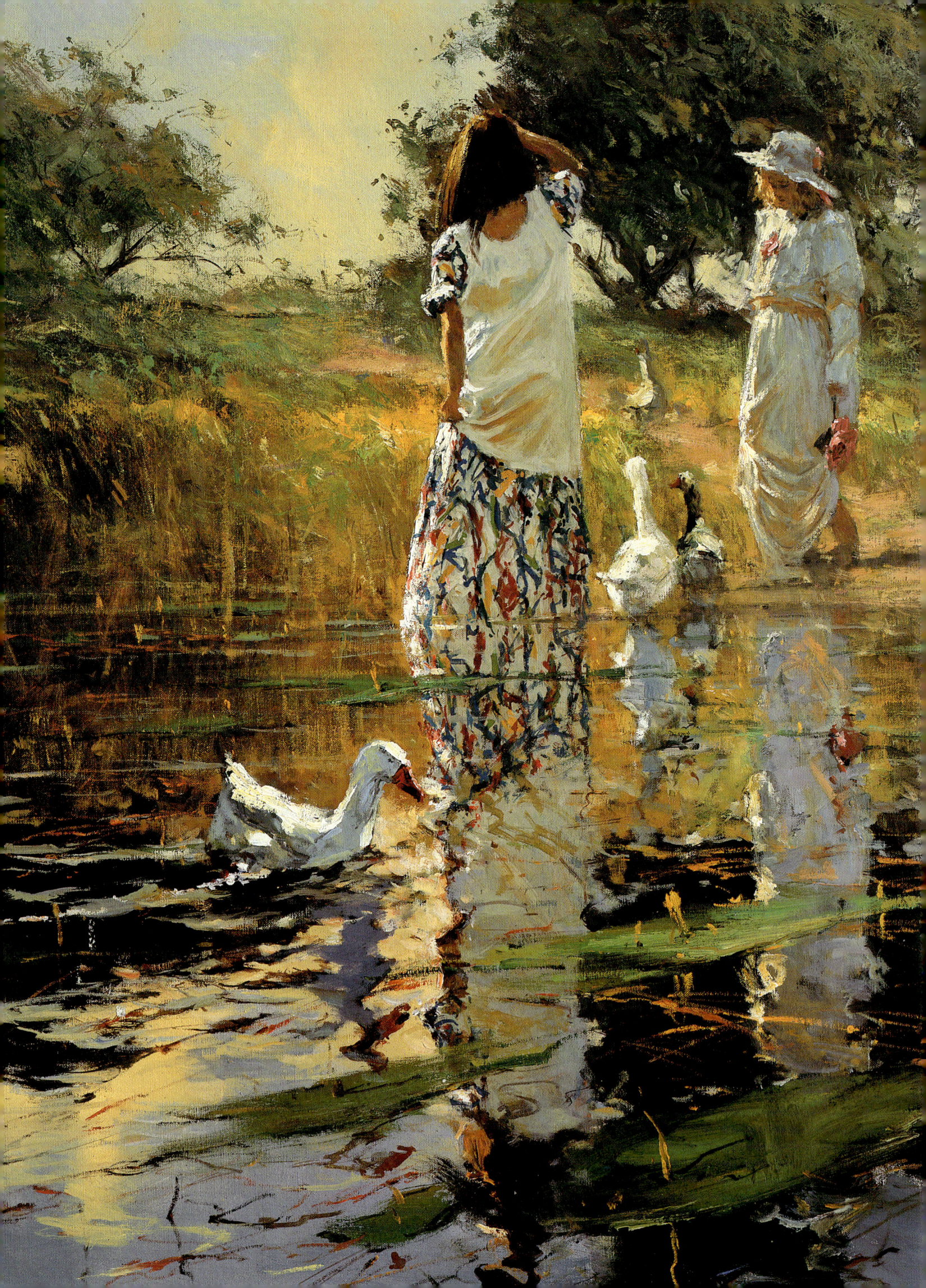

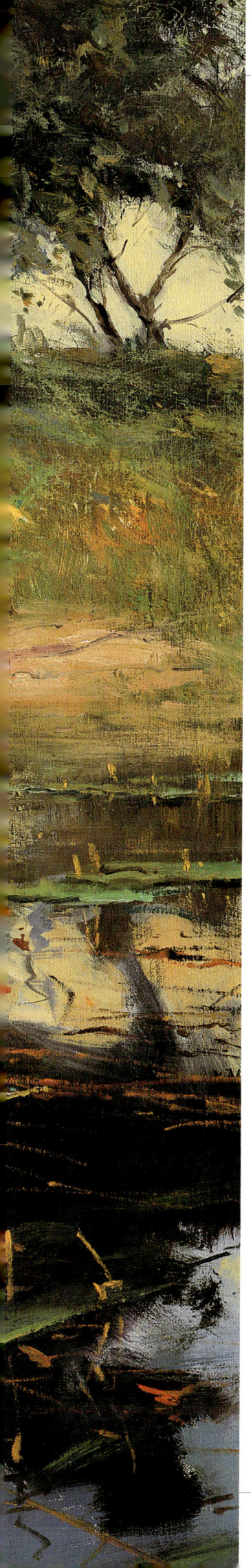

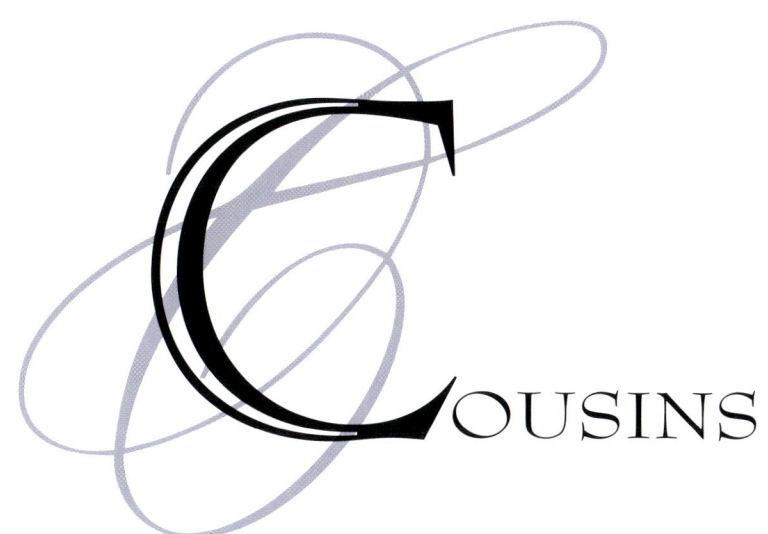 Cousins

Oh, the unclutter and innocence of cousins' first meeting...
Do you remember the excitement, the apprehension, what words to choose...your first impression, the perfect greeting.

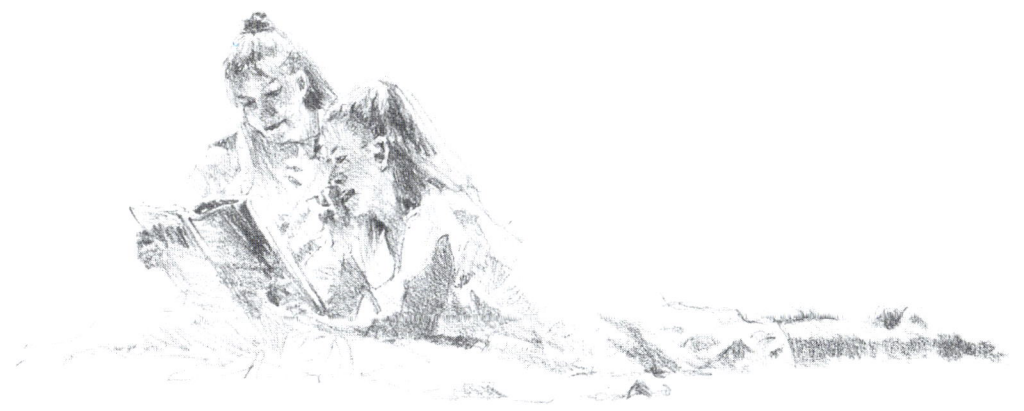

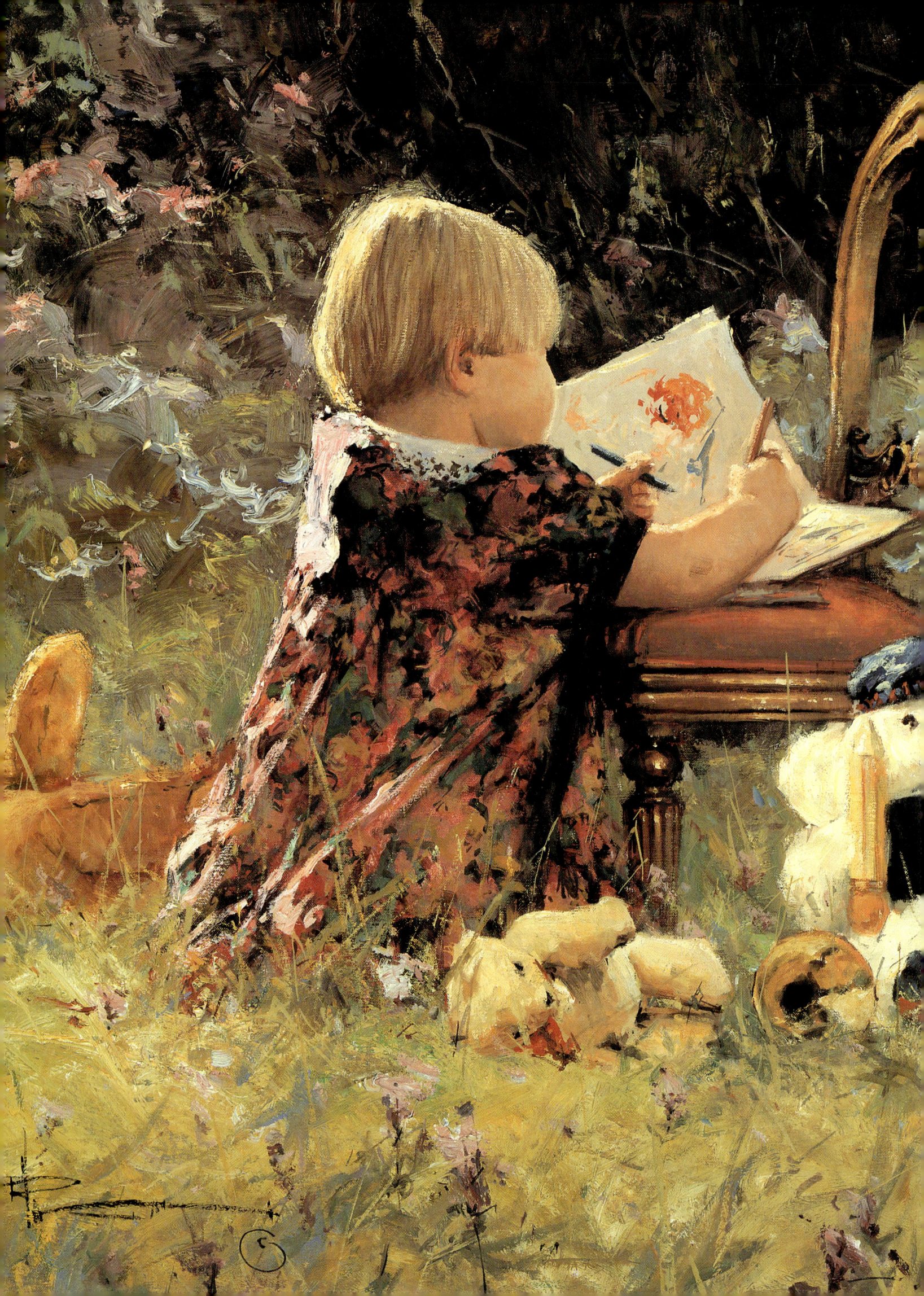

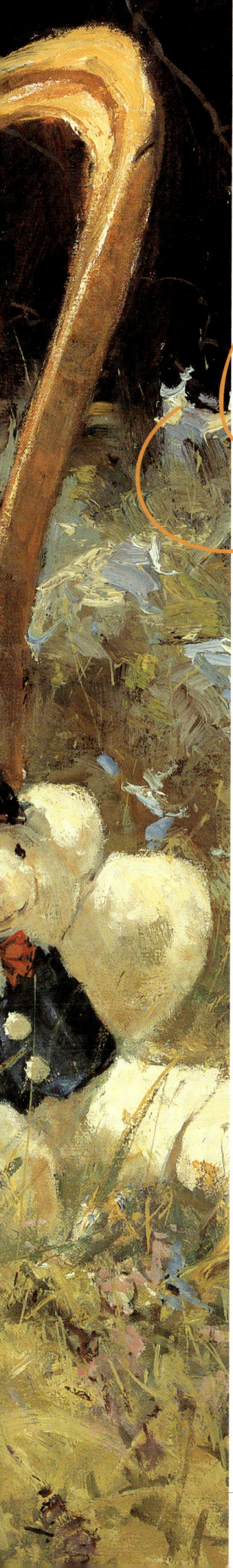

Teddy Time

The last time I took count, my four-year-old niece Belinda had somehow acquired a formidable family of exactly eleven teddy bears. As she has another birthday coming up pretty soon I guess I might as well buy her another one…if only for the sake of making her teddy tally an even dozen.

However, there's every chance that some of her several adoring uncles and aunts will have pretty much the same idea, so little Belinda's already large bear family could soon be dramatically larger still. This situation will cause her no problems whatever as she appears to be working on the theory that for a little girl there's no such thing as having too many teddies.

Belinda is an only child, at least so far, and this being the case, I suppose it's no great surprise that she's using teddy bears as playmate substitutes for the little brothers and sisters she doesn't have.

> "If I were a bear
> And a big bear, too
> I shouldn't much care
> If it froze or snew."
>
> —A. A. MILNE (WINNIE THE POOH, 1926)

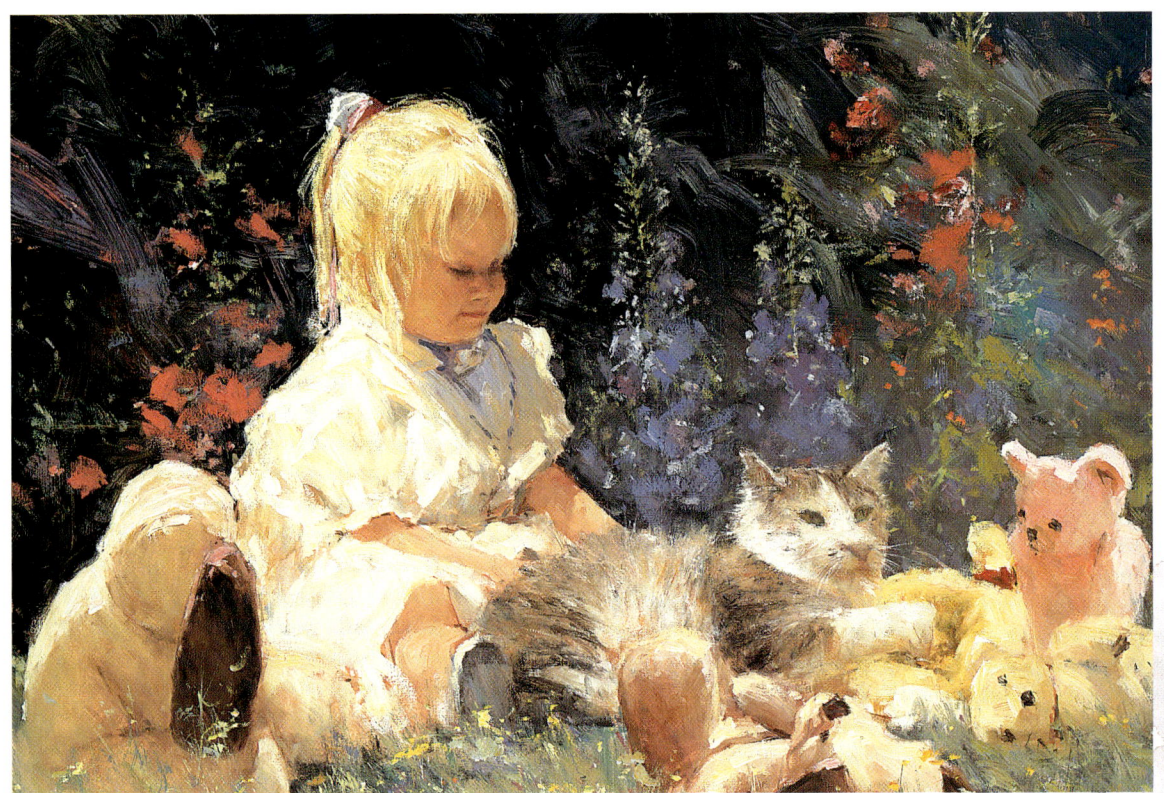

But she's still blessed by being a member of a very large family, by today's standards anyway. She is growing up with a Mom and a Daddy and surrounded by the protective affection of numerous very caring uncles and aunts, who all love her madly and will always be there for her.

It is interesting to reflect that over the last 30 years or so, there has been a gradual diminution of the family circle. The circle has become smaller and smaller until today, for millions of American children, just as it is in my home country, Australia, there's hardly a family circle at all. A small child affected by all this has no wide, comforting surrounding ring of uncles, aunts and cousins and it must make some of them feel so lonely and insecure and, possibly, rebellious.

So, as this is the prevailing social situation, I guess it's not hard to understand why so many kids nowadays are getting themselves into terrible trouble very early in life. I'm just glad that I was lucky enough to have been born at a time when large families were the rule rather than the rarity. That explains why I remember my own childhood with pleasant memories of being a part of a warm blanketing shelter of family affection.

As for my little niece Belinda and her teddy bear collection, well, if it's always another teddie she wants on her birthdays I'm happy to keep buying them for her for quite a few more years to come…or at least until she hollers uncle.

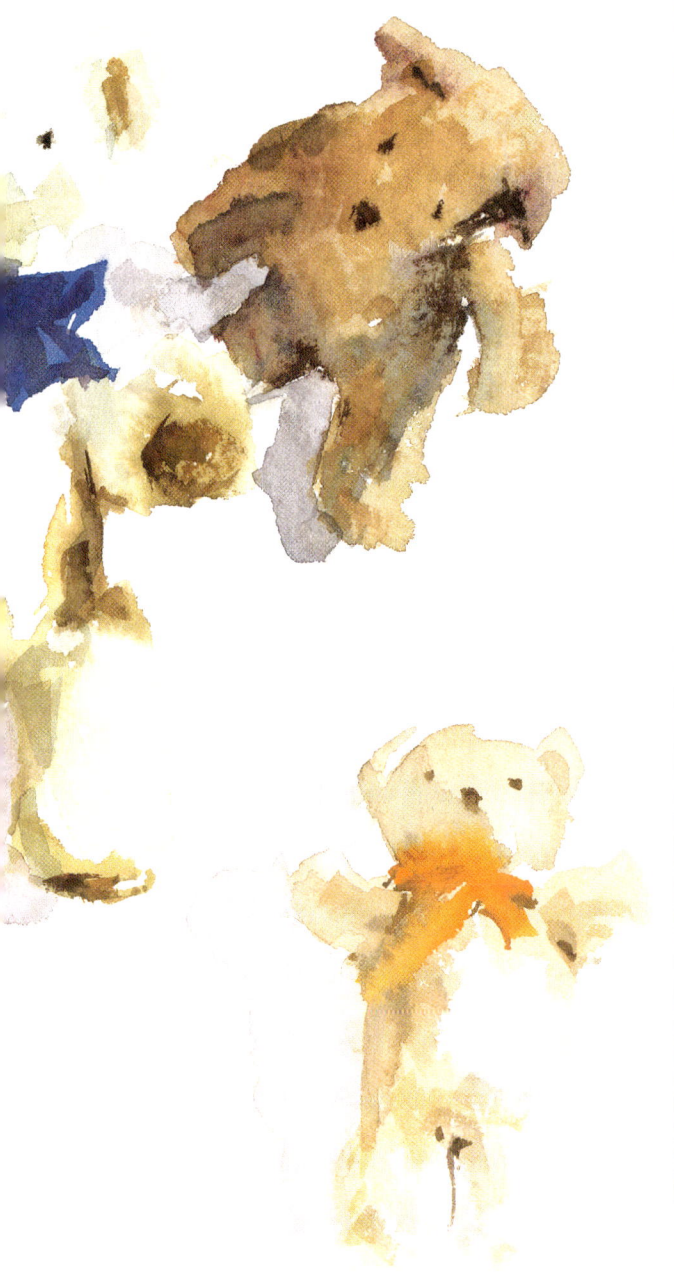

Why do they call them teddy bears? For some reason I'd always assumed that these cute little toys were originally associated with English children – the teddy bear is perhaps more popular in that country than anywhere else in the world. But I am now reliably informed, that the teddy was born right here in America, and in fact, all teddies are named after none other than Theodore "Teddy" Roosevelt, President of the United States from 1901 to 1909.

Apparently, a famous cartoon in the early 1900s depicted President Roosevelt saving the life of a bear cub while on a hunting expedition and ever since then millions and millions of stuffed little toy bears have been given the nickname, "Teddy."

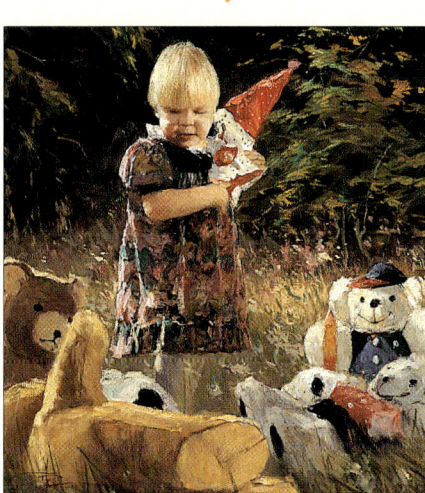

Life Renewing

Sometimes when I look at all the depressing scenes on the six o'clock TV news I begin to wonder if this weary old world has just about run its race. But fortunately, it doesn't take much to snap me out of this melancholy mood.

All I need to restore my fervent confidence in the future is a mere passing glance at some tangible evidence that, in spite of all the sad events unfolding everywhere, life still goes on – defiantly renewing itself. And the evidence is all around us, in countless wonderful forms…a lush green paddock full of frolicking new born lambs, a wobbly-legged calf vigorously suckling milk from a cow. Or it could be the especially beautiful evidence of a magnificent swan gliding gracefully across a stream with her little family of cygnets trailing dutifully behind.

There is also, of course, the ever-present human evidence that new life is about to spring forth in the world. A young woman, with the serene expression of expectant motherhood, is an undeniable fact that life just keeps rolling on…and on and on.

I've learned that to be privileged to observe the myriad forms of new life emerging before our eyes is something we should never take for granted.

Years ago, I was a member of a small group of artists volunteering to visit a state penitentiary to give a course of art lessons to selected prisoners. It was through these prison visits that the expression "life renewing itself" took on a much deeper meaning for me. I often had lengthy conversations with some of the prisoners attending the art lessons and they would quite freely talk about the hardships of prison life and the things they missed most by being removed from society.

One of the prisoners, a really tough looking character with scars on his face and heavily tattooed arms, surprised me by admitting that it wasn't so much the saloons and the womenfolk that he missed the most – it was children, not just his own, but all children. "That's the one thing that just about all the guys in here all agree on," he said. "They miss seein' little kids runnin' around and hearin' em laughin' – Once you're locked away from kids for a while you just don't realize how much ya miss 'em. And it really gets ya low. When there ain't no kids around ya can't see the future in anything, can ya?"

And the irony about that statement is that the prisoner who said that to me…was serving a life sentence.

To plant seeds, and watch the renewal of life
This is the commonest delight of the race.
—Charles Dudley Warner
(1829–1900)

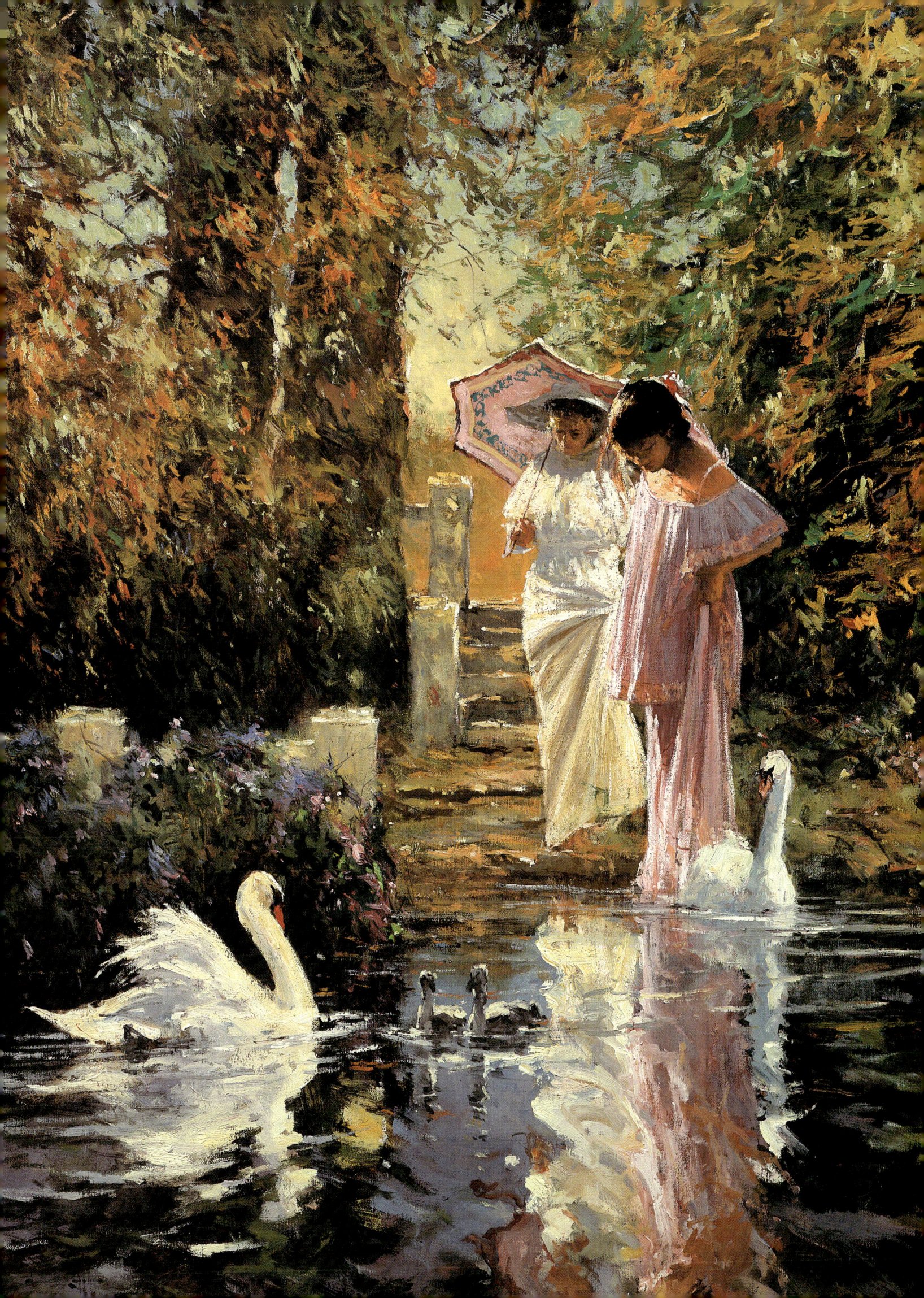

Joy of Spring

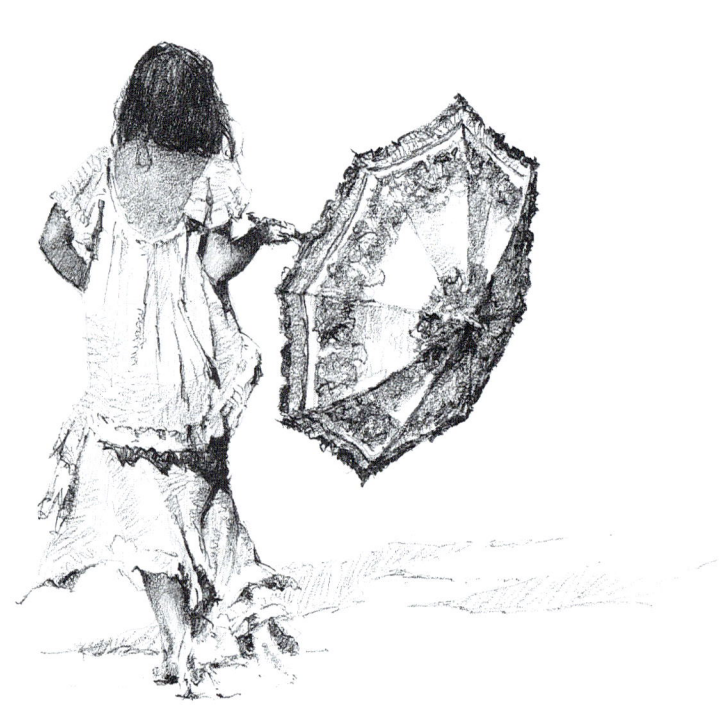

If winter comes
Can Spring be far behind?

— Shelley

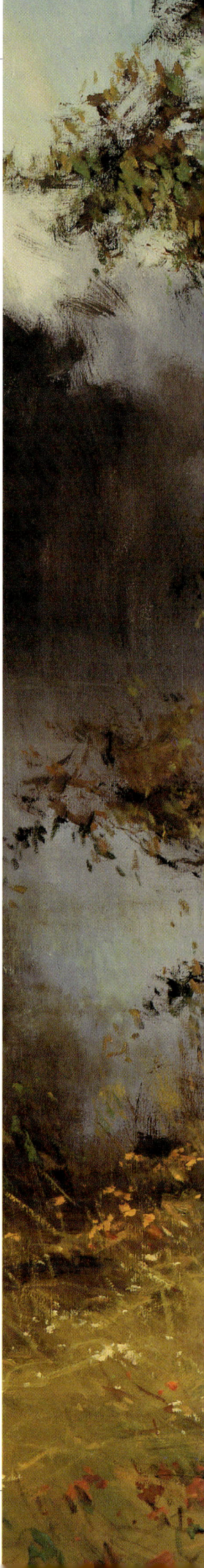

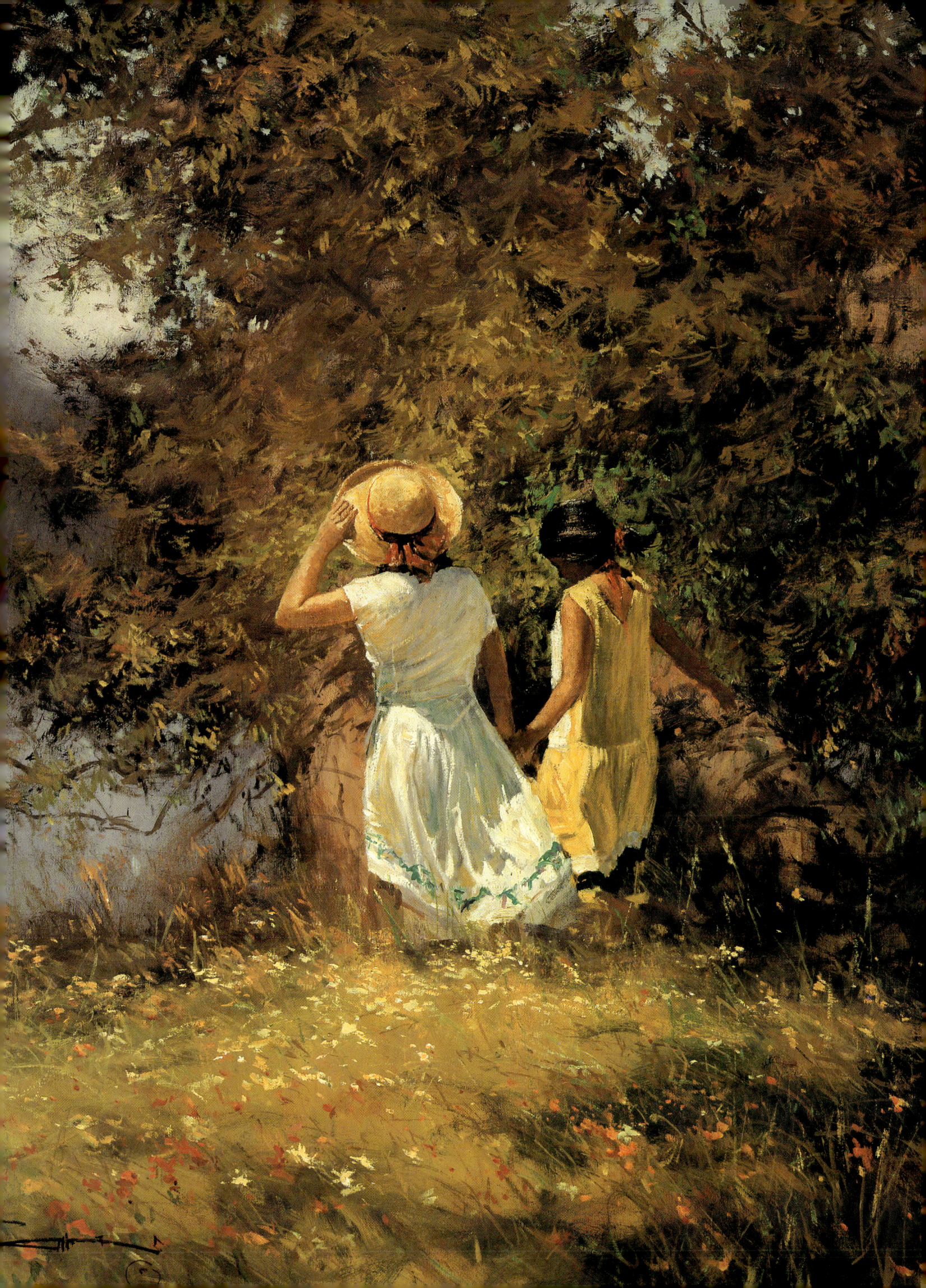

A Cherished Memory

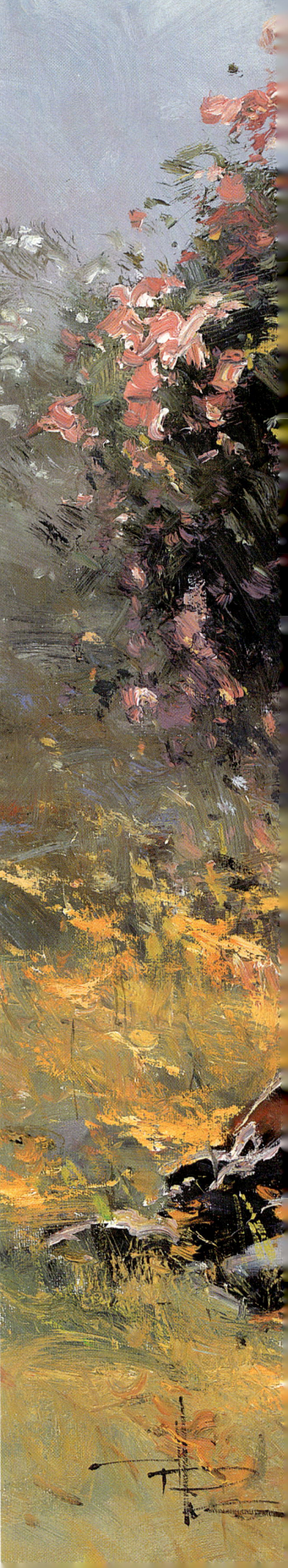

Whenever I find I have some spare time I give art lessons in my San Diego studio to the wives of a few local business acquaintances of mine. The ladies are all quite enthusiastic hobby artists and these little group instructional sessions are relaxed and informal. We all have a very pleasant time.

I prefer not to be too intrusive, so I just look over their shoulders to help with a little technical tip now and again. However, like most amateur artists, they often have problems deciding on their painting subjects and this is one area where I can give them more serious professional guidance.

At a recent art class I suggested to them one way to ensure they really enjoy their painting hobby was to paint subjects that evoke pleasing personal memories. Some happy early childhood memory, perhaps?

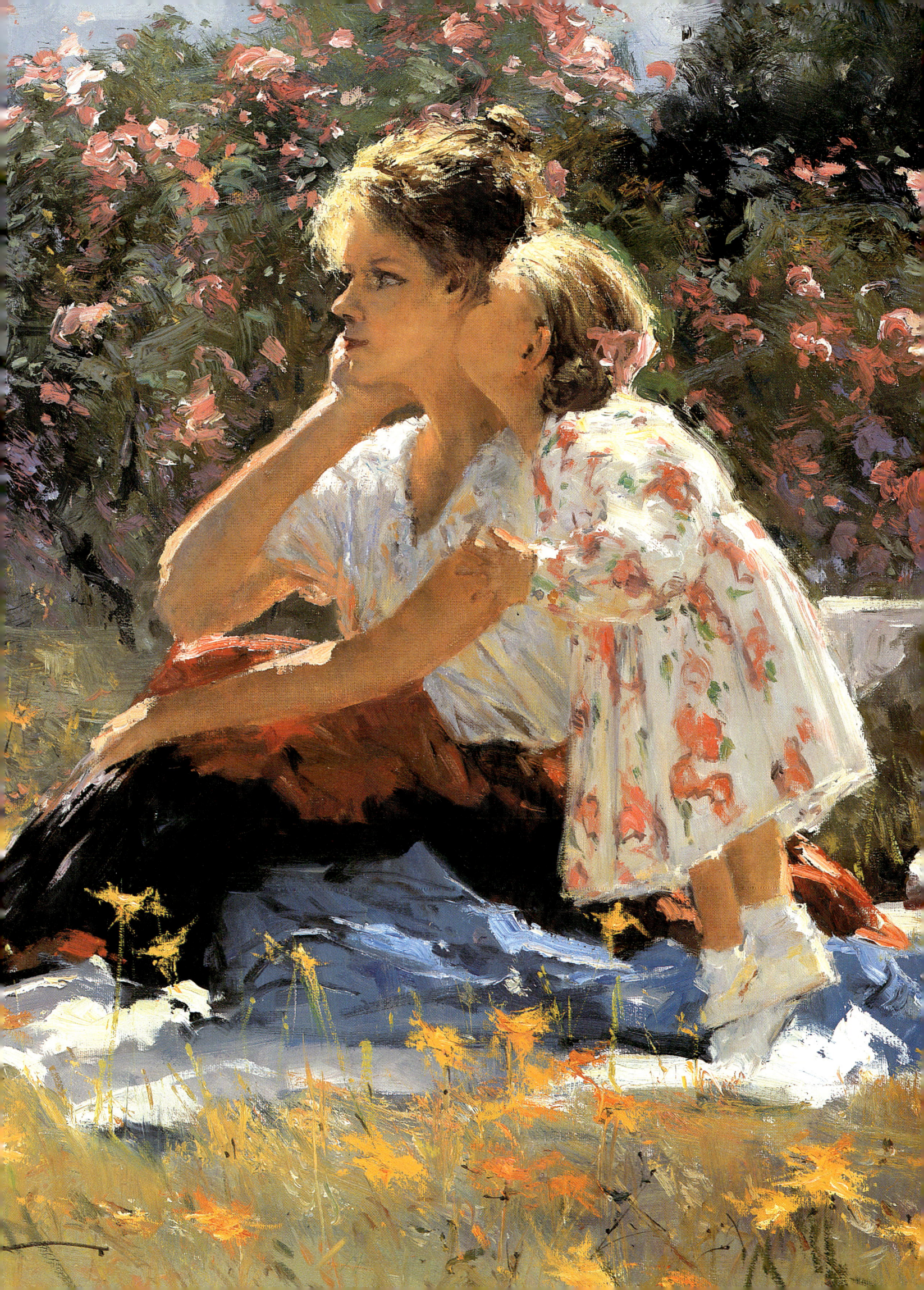

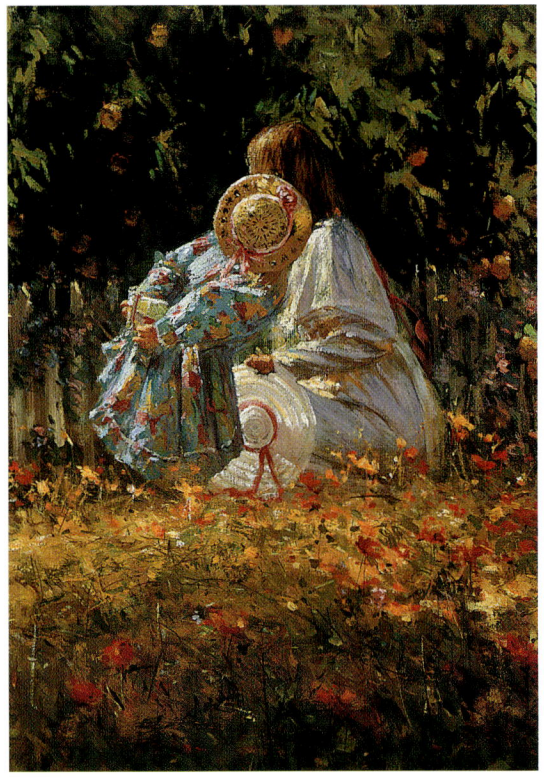

This set them to thinking and they all came up with various mental images of their childhood years that suddenly inspired them all to put brush to canvas. They were painting all kinds of cherished memories from their childhood days – making a sand castle on the beach, a favorite pony from the farm…one lady even painted herself as a child buying an ice cream from the corner store.

Julie, one of the older ladies in my class, confessed that her childhood years were in the 1940s and that her most pleasant memory from around that time was of her parents' lovely little country cottage in Southern California where she was born. Naturally, I thought this would make an excellent painting subject and I suggested that she start on it immediately. But then Julie surprised me with a most unusual request – she didn't feel that she was sufficiently experienced in her newly embarked painting hobby to do it justice. So she wanted me to paint her family's cottage for her!

Well, this really floored me. It's hard enough even for professional artists to transfer their own distant memories accurately onto the canvas, but to try to recreate someone else's very personal childhood recollection? This seemed like a no-win situation.

Fortunately, she made the assignment a little bit easier for me. "It's not the house so much that I remember," she admitted, "it was just a little white-walled cottage with a red roof and a chimney, but I mainly recall the big tree out front, so just put the house in the background and concentrate on the big tree."

That simplified matters to some degree, so in the background goes one small white cottage, red roof with chimney. Now for the tree.

"It was an orange tree," Julie advised me. "It was a big orange tree that had branches spreading right out in front of the house, and I really loved that old tree. Can the tree dominate the picture?"

Again, no problem. One orange tree coming up. Julie remembered that in springtime her tree was always loaded down with plump juicy California oranges, so I painted lots of oranges hanging from every bough. This wasn't turning out too difficult at all.

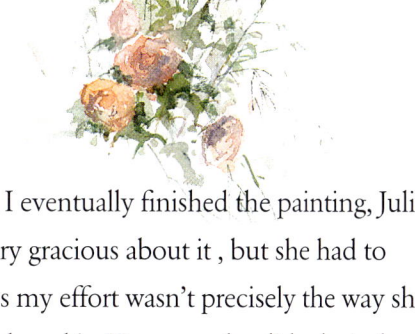

"That looks about right," she said when I'd finished, "but there was to be a white picket fence alongside it and the branches would hang down, lovingly, right over that little fence."

On goes the picket fence, as instructed. And this is when my recreation of her cherished memory ran into a spot of quicksand.

"It's…kinda like it," she said, sounding a little unconvincing, "but there's something else I want you to add to the painting…and I really don't know how you're going to handle this."

Neither did I. But, well, try me, I told her. Whatever it is I'll at least give it my best shot.

"It's my mother," said Julie hesitantly." I remember it was her birthday and I was just a little girl, about four or five, and I ran up to her in front of the picket fence in my best blue party dress and I gave her a little present."

She was right – I certainly didn't know how to handle it! Without even a faded family album photograph to help me, how could I possibly continue? But guided by Julie's somewhat hazy description I somehow soldiered on.

When I eventually finished the painting, Julie was very gracious about it , but she had to confess my effort wasn't precisely the way she remembered it. However, she did admit that it was near enough to rekindle a very precious memory of one of the happiest days of her childhood.

And I guess, if a painting achieves that alone, for just one person, then it has certainly served its purpose.

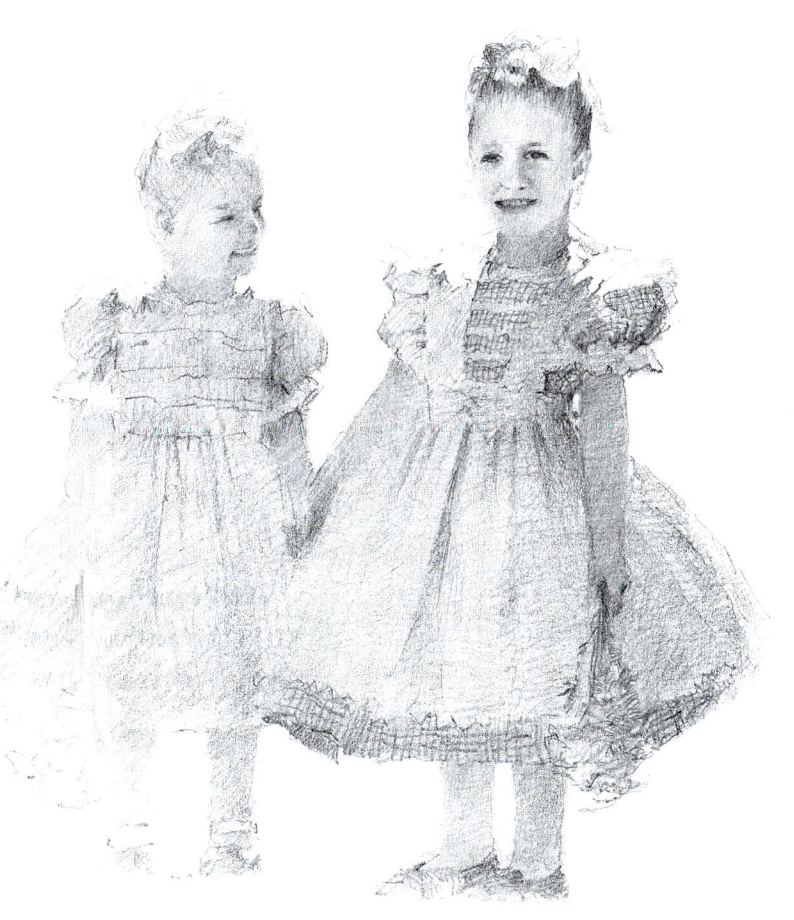

Life

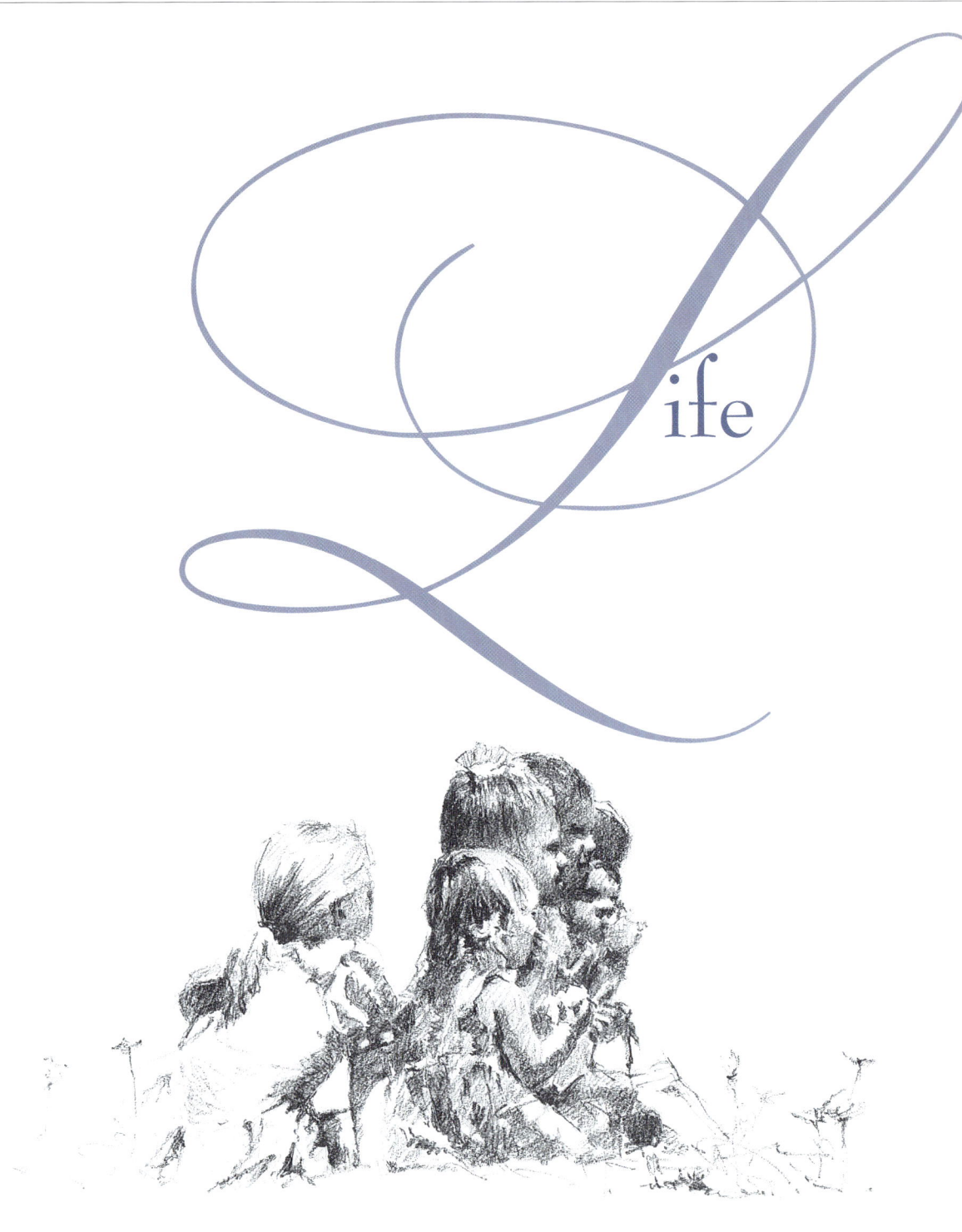

Flowers are lovely
Love is a flower - like
Friendship is a sheltering tree
Oh the joys that came down shower - like
Of Friendship, love and liberty
Ere I was old.

— SAMUEL TAYLOR COLERIDGE
(1772–1834)

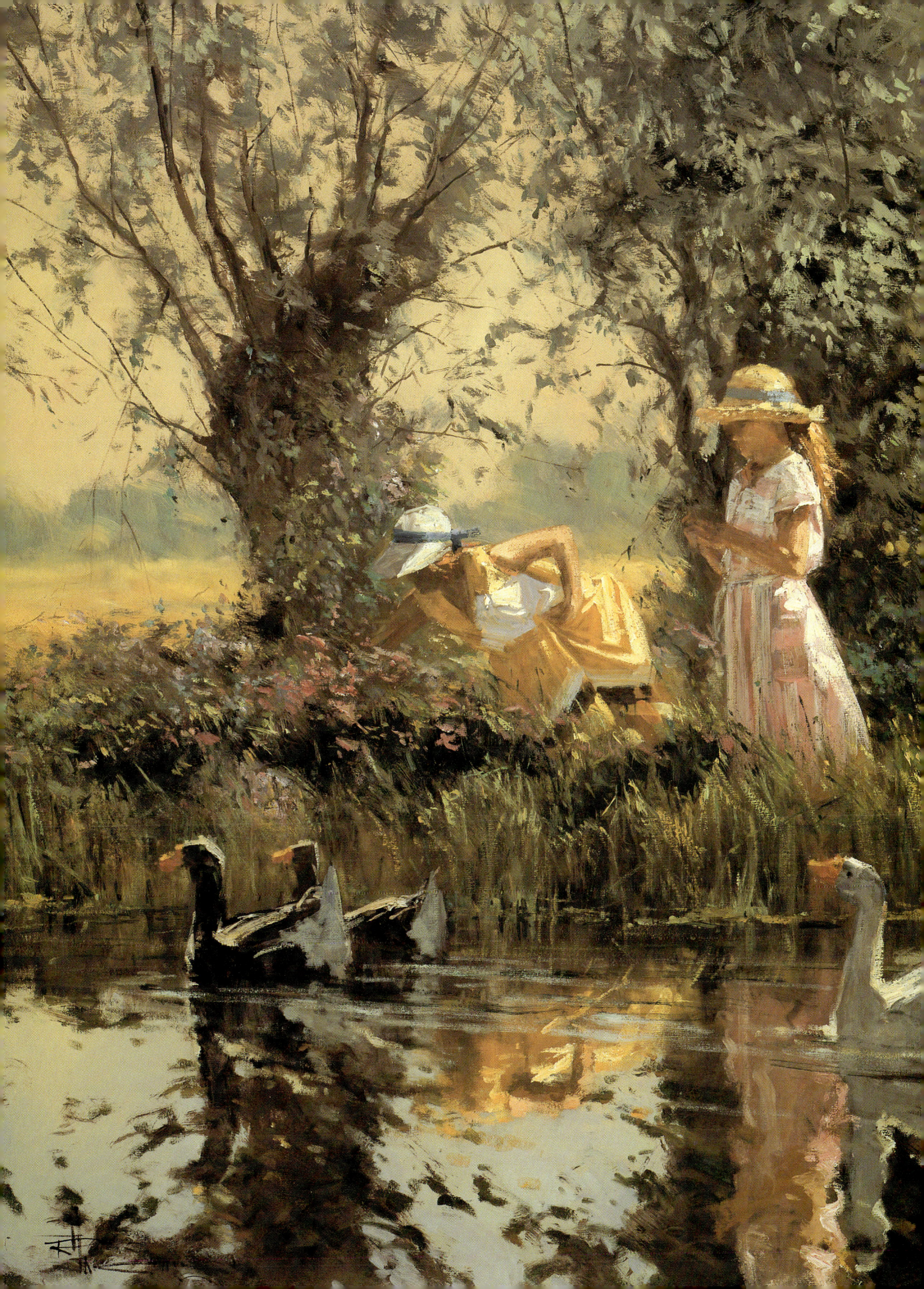

Running Free

Just a simple rural scene of a carefree little girl chasing geese into a stream on the family farm. It is a timeless, everyday scene of a happy child at play.

Whenever I've exhibited a painting in some way similar to the one on the page opposite, I'm occasionally asked by onlookers why I decided to paint anything as simple and meaningless as say – a little girl chasing geese.

Frankly, I'm always at a loss to come up with a very satisfactory answer to such a question, except to counter with the old rejoiner that what may seem meaningless to one beholder may have a very tangible meaning to someone else.

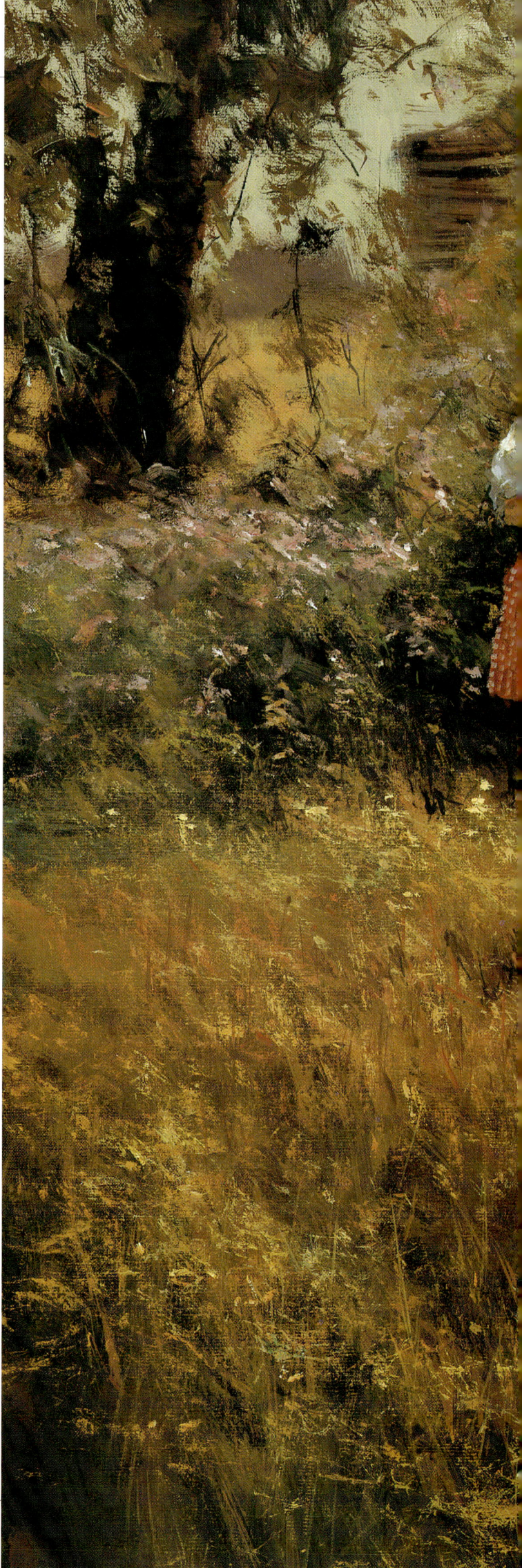

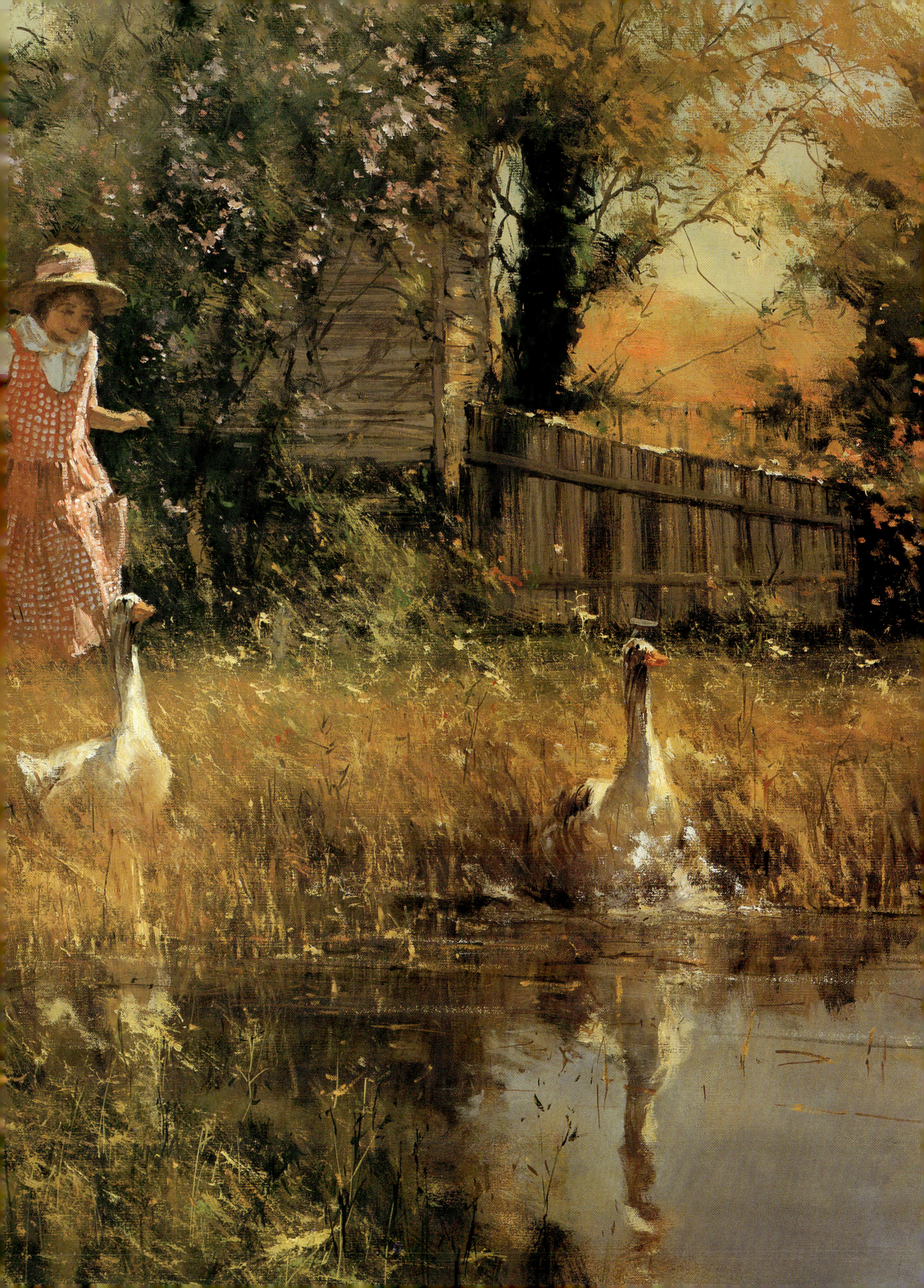

However, for whatever it's worth, I can truthfully state that there is always a little story of some kind behind every painting I produce, and there happens to be a very joyful and inspiring story associated with this particular painting. The little girl running after the geese is a real person named Jennifer and the fact that she is able to run at all is, in itself, more than sufficient and meaningful motivation for the creation of this painting.

Jennifer is well known to me because she's the seven-year-old daughter of two close friends of mine. On the day that she was born I helped her Dad to celebrate the great event in his life, so in a way I feel I'm one of the little girl's unofficial Godfathers. Anyway, the story behind Jennifer is her courageous struggle to overcome the tough time she had to endure very early in life.

It happened this way. When she was about three years old, she suddenly ran out into the street chasing a little colored ball of hers and got hit by a car. The accident could have been a lot worse, the front fender of the car merely clipped her legs. When she was x-rayed it seemed that she had only suffered simple fractures. Later, it was discovered, the fractures were not so simple at all.

For some very complicated medical reasons her little bones refused to knit properly and she spent the next four years on and off in various hospitals, undergoing many operations and having to endure a great deal of pain and loneliness. Fortunately, as my painting reveals, there is a very happy ending to this story.

She eventually made such a complete recovery she was able to throw away her leg calipers and experience the exhilaration of chasing pet geese when she visited her grandparents' farm.

A meaningless painting? On the surface, perhaps it is. But it is possible to read all kinds of meanings into any painting, and I hope it means quite a lot to the parents whose children have regained good health after suffering serious illness or injuries in their lives. Meaningless? To some, I guess it is, but possibly there are many loving parents who will work out their own meanings behind such a painting.

> "This year's at the spring
>
> And day's at the mourn
>
> Morning's at seven
>
> The hillside's dew-pear led
>
> The lark's on the wing
>
> The snail's on the thorn
>
> God's in His heaven
>
> All's right with the world."
>
> — ROBERT BROWNING (1812–1889)

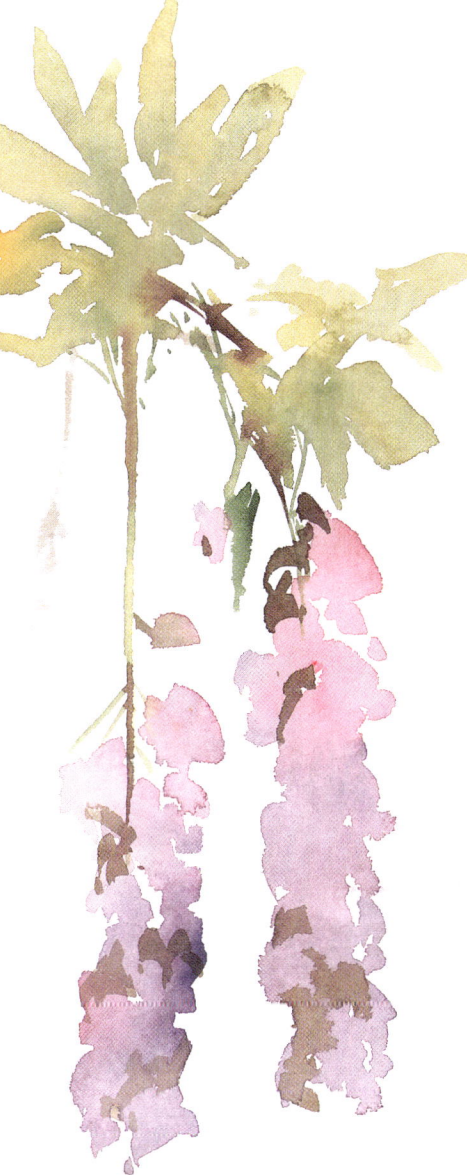

Buttercup Secrets

Will you just look at those two. There they are again, with their heads together, totally engrossed in each other's foolish little secrets. Calmly oblivious to the rest of the world with all its rioting and mayhem.

The spring is in the meadow and the buttercups are out. And, like countless generations of young girls before them down through the centuries, they're out in the meadow picking buttercups and telling each other their most private dreams and desires. Buttercups, the flower for young girls and the flower to symbolize a young girl's secrets.

But what is her secret worth if she has no one to share it? Look at those two again…thirteen-year-old school girls, best friends, on vacation and having fun, and what is it they are whispering to each other? Whatever it is…it is for their ears only.

It doesn't even matter if you happen to overhear them for they speak in a strange secret language all their own that only they can understand. They live in a secret world with barriers drawn against all grown-ups, and if you dare intrude on that secret world you are met with frowning brows, pouting lips and a sudden icy cold silence.

It is wise not to intrude. It is best to keep your distance.

So when you see them together, strolling by, whispering, giggling, whispering again. Don't call out, don't break the spell. They're only thirteen, after all, and very soon life will catch up with them, and they'll have to go their separate ways.

The secret years are fleeting.

> "Someone to confide in
>
> A friend to share those private thoughts
>
> Someone with a kindly ear
>
> A friend to share those troubled times"
>
> — CAROLYN WELLS (1847–1898)

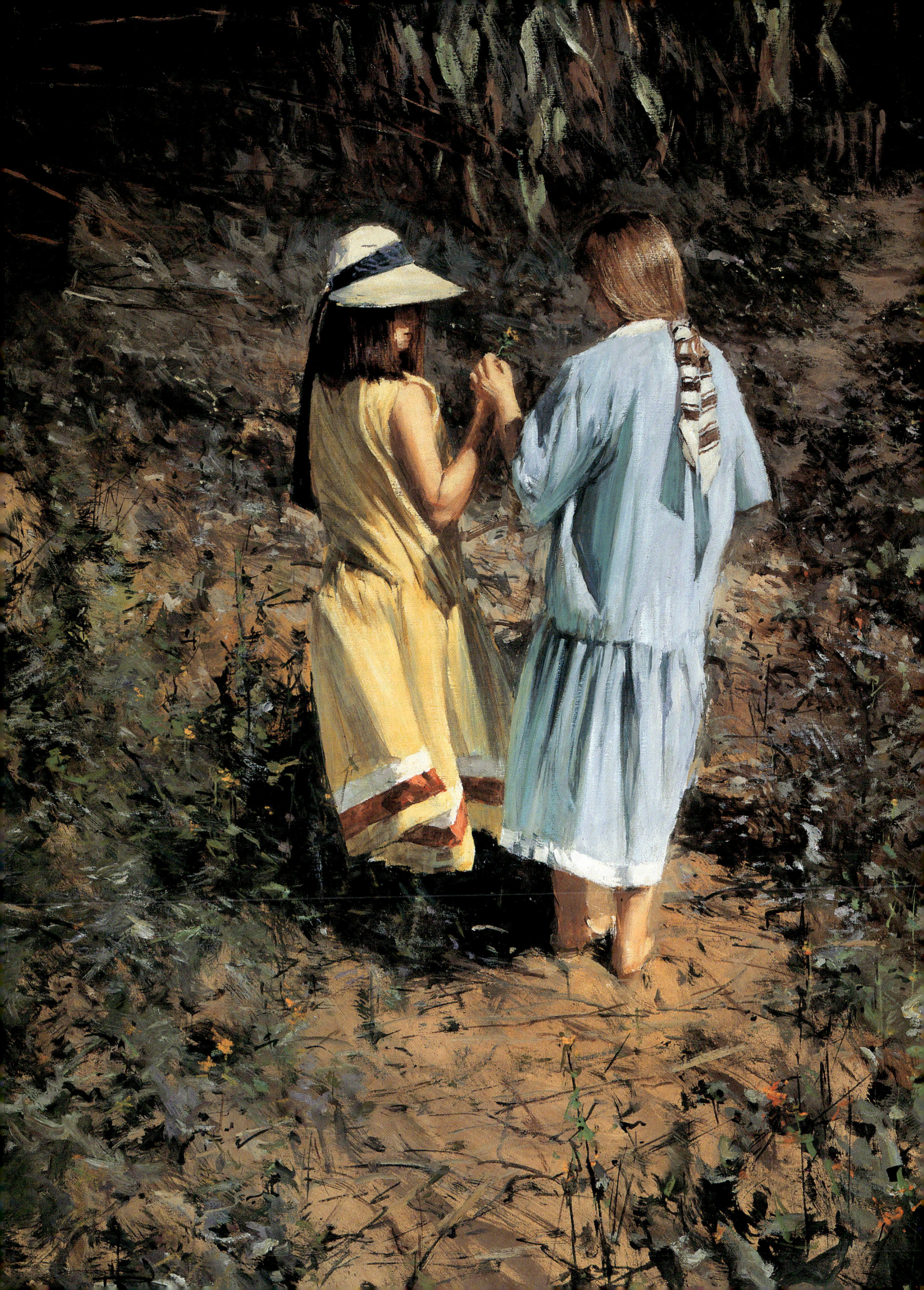

Prized Shell

I suppose there are more pleasing sights than children happily at play on a beach, earnestly building sand castles and keenly discovering shells. But offhand I can't think of a single one.

Children are at their happiest on the seashore. Their shining eyes as they delve into the sand with buckets and little spades, their delighted squeals as the waves lap around their ankles. These are the sunny, precious moments of childhood.

Even as they grow older a child's fascination with seashells continues. But eventually the child must become an adult and adults refrain from picking up shells. Though the fascination is still there, the adult feels too embarrassed to stoop and pick up the shell. It is a childish thing to do.

A child scurries past the beach-walkers
And runs to the water's edge
The child is innocent
Free of inhibitions.
And searching for seashells.

> But I have sinuous shells of pearly hue
> Shake one, and it awakens; then apply
> It's polished lips to your attentive ear
> And it remembers its august abodes
> And murmurs as the ocean murmurs there.
>
> — WALTER SAVAGE LANDOR
> (1775–1864)

A pearly shell
That murmurs of the
far-off Murmuring sea

A precious jewel
Carved most curiously
It is a little picture
Painted well.

— RICHARD
WATSON
GILDER
(1844–1909)

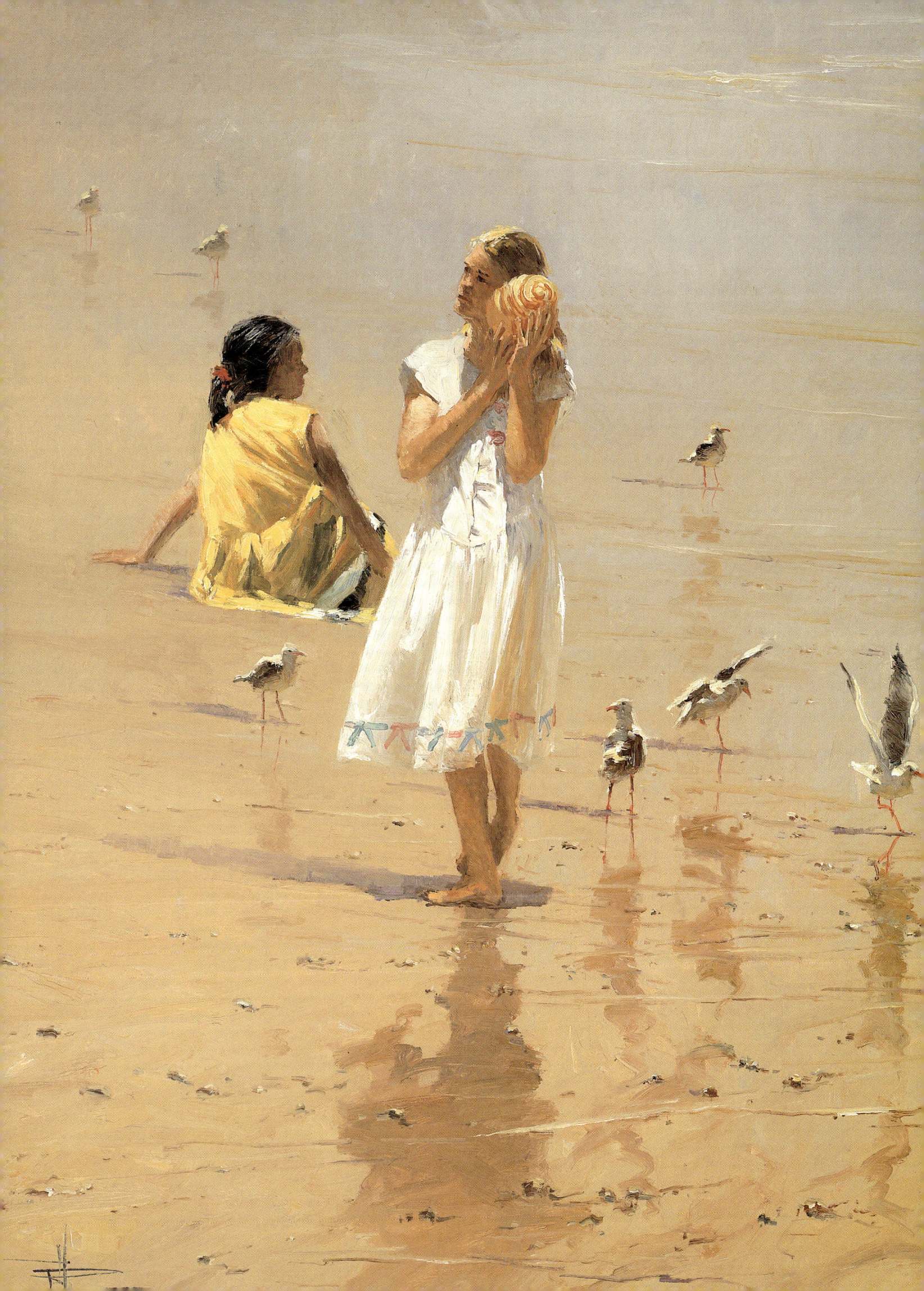

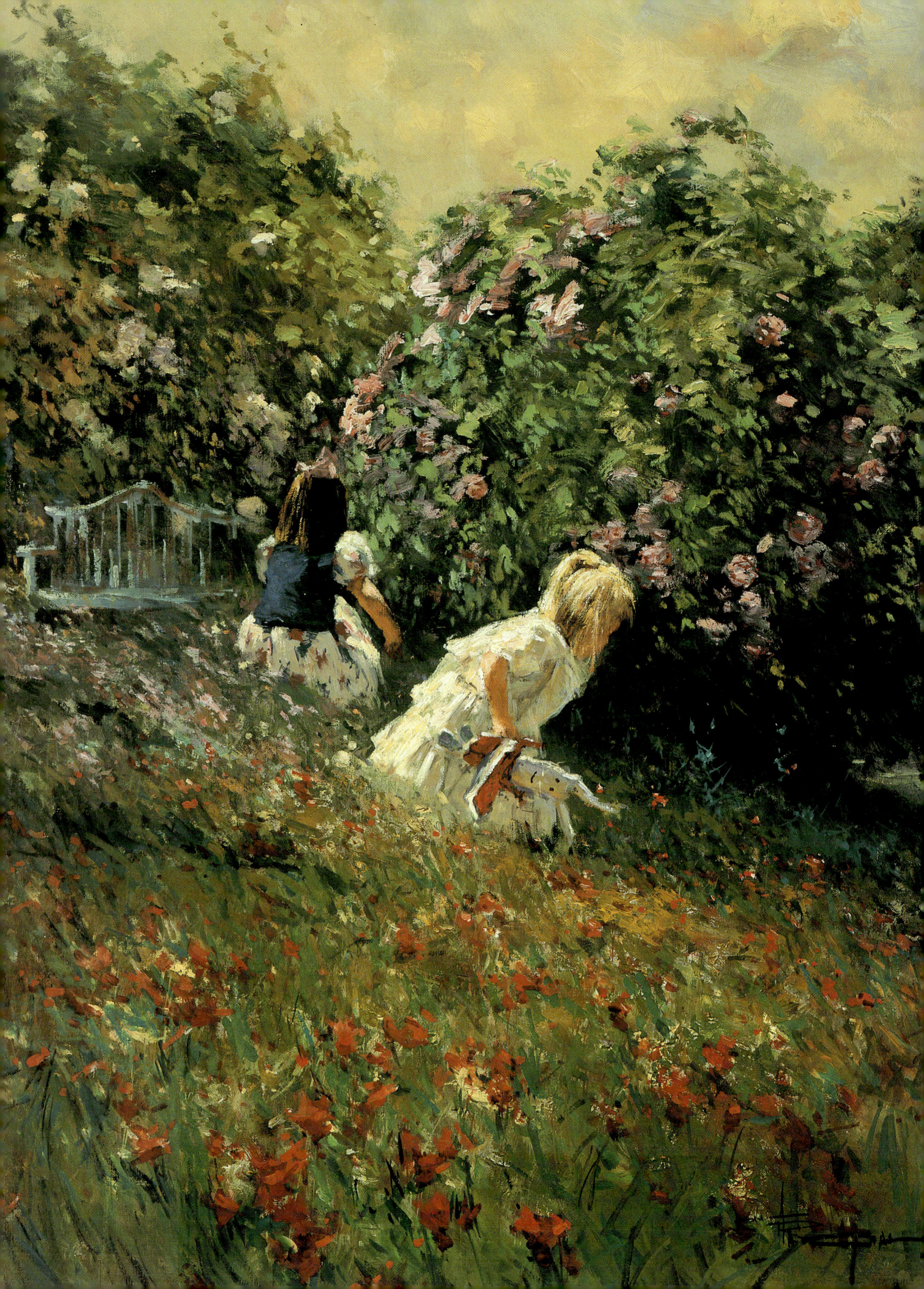

Country Wildflowers

To behold your children picking flowers in a country field is to witness one of life's most charming rituals. And to be presented with a gift of wildflowers from your shining-eyed little ones is surely one of life's treasures.

City children romping free in a country paddock among the farm animals and the wildflowers are children suddenly unleashed to the wonders of nature. How thrilled they always are when told the news that they are about to be taken for a drive to the country to visit family friends or relatives. Despite all the modern high-tech diversions now available, such as endless variations of computer games, there's nothing like a trip out to the country to get the kids really excited.

I consider myself fortunate, indeed, that I happened to be raised in a small country village, and as a result I have countless marvelous memories of those rural days. The sights, the sounds and, yes, even the smells of country life are still clearly retained in my mind.

The rolling green hills, the stony-bottomed creeks, the lowing herds of cattle, the frolicking new-born lambs… Those of us who left all that behind seeking success in the rat-race of the city may not altogether regret the big move, but we certainly never forget our country roots.

To see a world in a grain of sand

And a heaven in a wildflower

Hold infinity in the palm of your hand

And eternity in an hour.

— WILLIAM BLAKE
(1757–1827)

I take my children out to the country as often as I can because, well, it may be just a personal bias, but I don't want them to grow up entirely ignorant of country life. I want them to at least occasionally rub a horse's nose, feed corn to backyard chickens and get out and play amongst forest trees and hillside flowers. In other words, I want to get them a little bit countrified.

I want them to hear the raucous calling of the hovering crows, to be able to look up and see a great big sky, in all its widespread glory, and not just some skinny filtered shaft of smoggy gray cloud lurking somewhere between the skyscrapers – the way it sadly is for them in the city.

To be countrified means to take things a little bit slower, a little bit easier. There's an old saying about how we should always take time to smell the flowers as we go through life. Perhaps we should not only take time to smell the flower – we should also pause a little longer, and touch its petals.

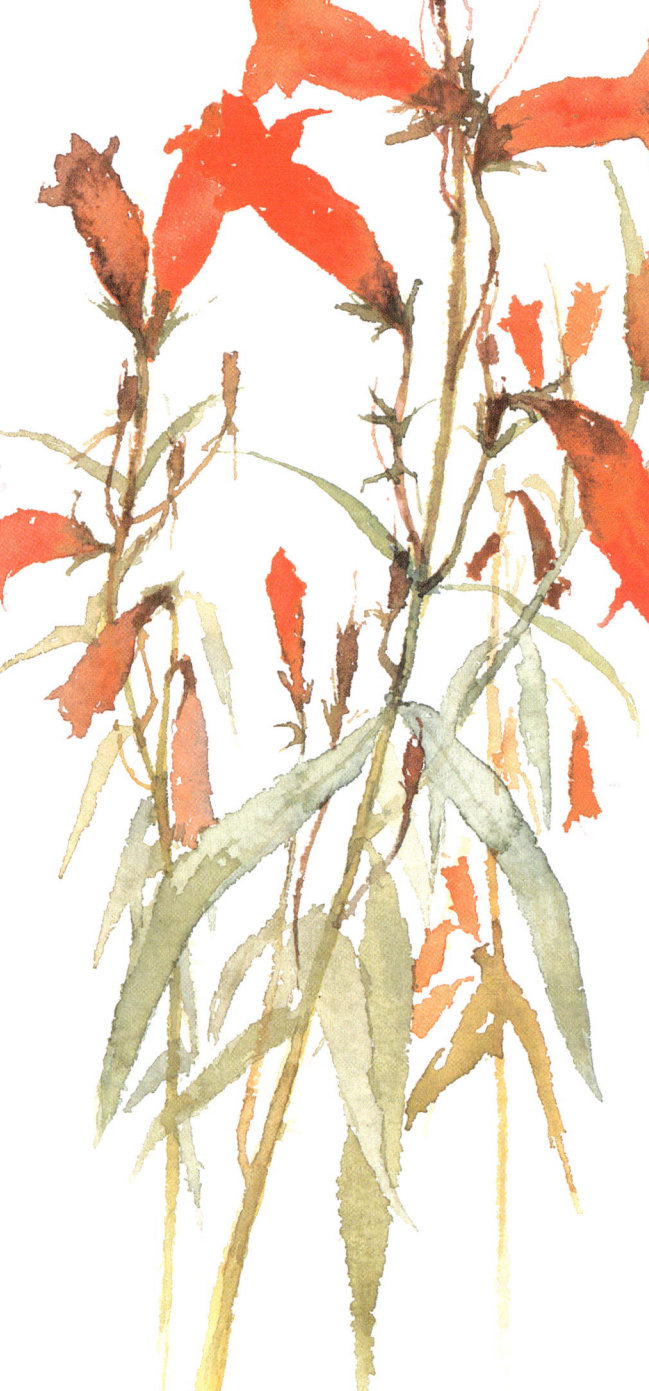

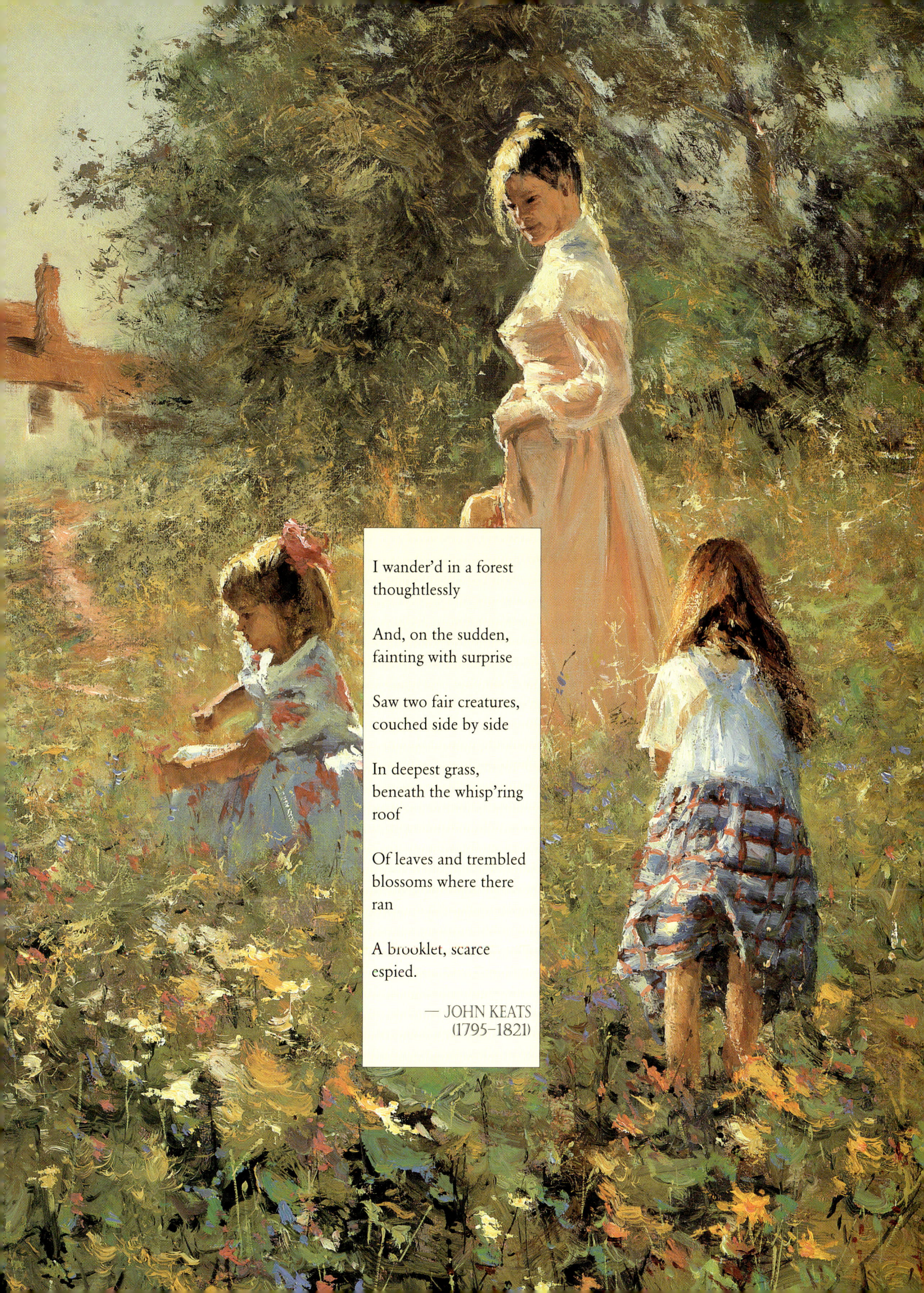

I wander'd in a forest thoughtlessly

And, on the sudden, fainting with surprise

Saw two fair creatures, couched side by side

In deepest grass, beneath the whisp'ring roof

Of leaves and trembled blossoms where there ran

A brooklet, scarce espied.

— JOHN KEATS
(1795–1821)

Rusty Comes Home

I want to tell you about a little dog called Rusty who belongs to Mike and Liz, friends of mine from way back, and the really surprising story about how Rusty came to be a part of their family. Now, Rusty is by no means a dog with a pedigree, in fact, if you asked Mike and Liz what breed Rusty is, it's like asking them to explain Einstein's theory of relativity. They've got a rough idea, but they're not quite sure. Under pressure they'll suddenly declare in well practiced unison, "He's a Jack Russell."

Well, I happen to be fairly familiar with the Jack Russell breed – they're exceptionally brave and intelligent little dogs with a couple of distinctive features. After a cursory inspection of Rusty I could tell that, yes indeed, there's definitely a touch of JR somewhere in his ancestry. Possibly there's a touch of whippet and fox terrier in there as well, but I thought it impolite to mention this. One reason I was sure about the JR link to Rusty's heritage was the fact that these cute little dogs tend to kick their hind legs in a funny way when running. And, sure enough, when Rusty was darting about in the back yard, his little back legs were kicking back in classic JR style.

Rusty was discovered by Mike and Liz when they took their two daughters, aged twelve and ten, to visit their old Uncle Jake, who lived alone on a small farm about twenty miles away. Uncle Jake always had a few dogs for company, and this time he had an extra one that he really didn't need. It had just wandered in from nowhere and the other dogs didn't seem to mind, so he'd sort of moved in and made himself at home. This little dog was Rusty, he was about six months old back then and still pretty much a playful pup.

> "Therefore to this dog will I
>
> Tenderly not scornfully
>
> Render praise and favor
>
> With my hand upon his head
>
> Is my benediction said
>
> Therefore and forever"
>
> — Elizabeth Barrett Browning (1806–1861) (to her dog, Flush)

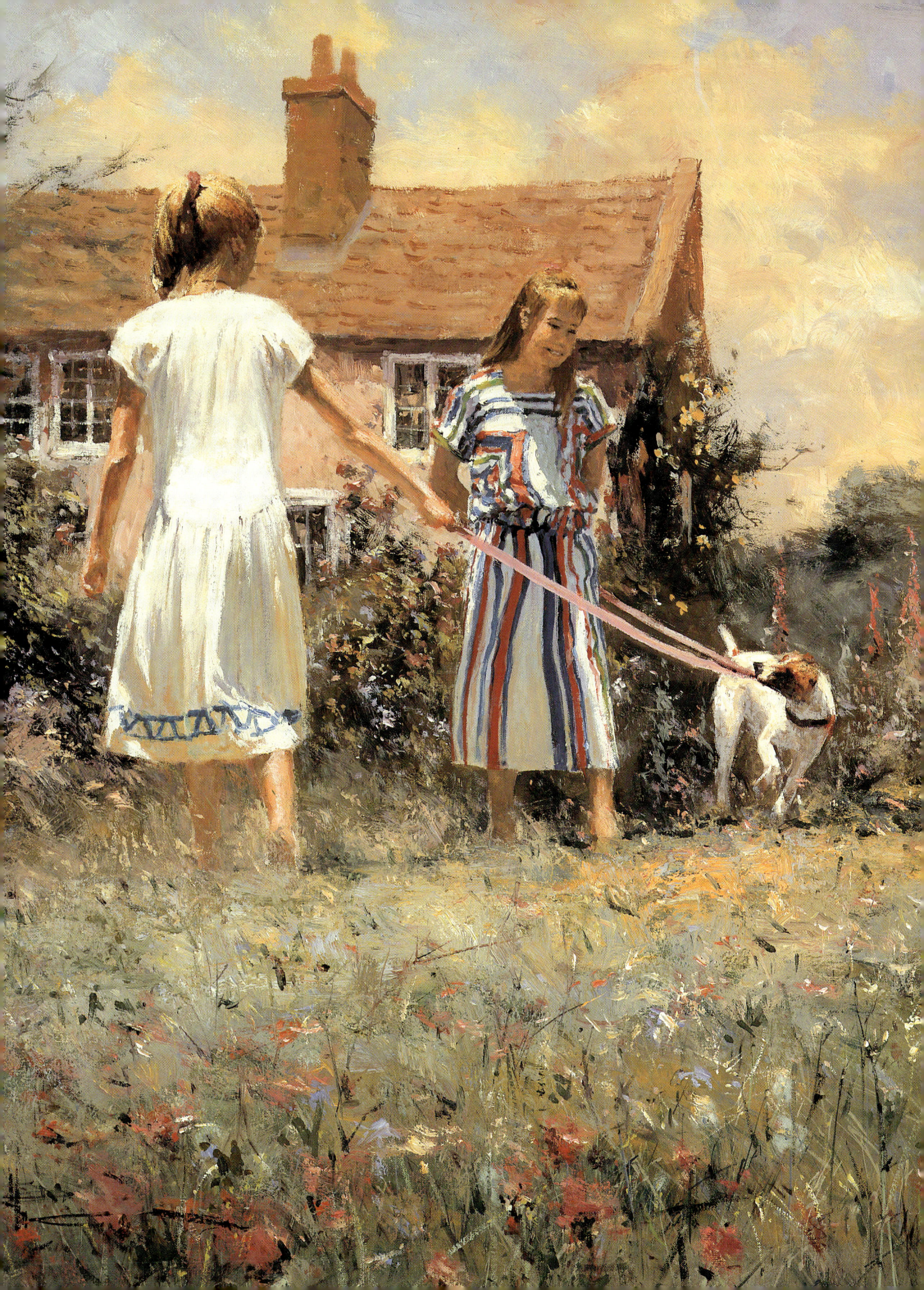

Well, Rusty was such a cute little fella that the two little girls hit it off with him straight away and they played with him all day long on their visit to the farm. When it came time to leave, Uncle Jake suggested to Mike and Liz that they could keep the dog if they wanted to. But they'd only moved into their new house and weren't prepared to take in the dog quite yet.

So the girls gave little Rusty a goodbye hug, got into the car with their parents and drove off.

Well, I imagine by now you've already guessed that by some miracle little Rusty managed to follow their car the entire twenty miles and eventually turned up on their front doorstep looking very bedraggled and sorry for himself.

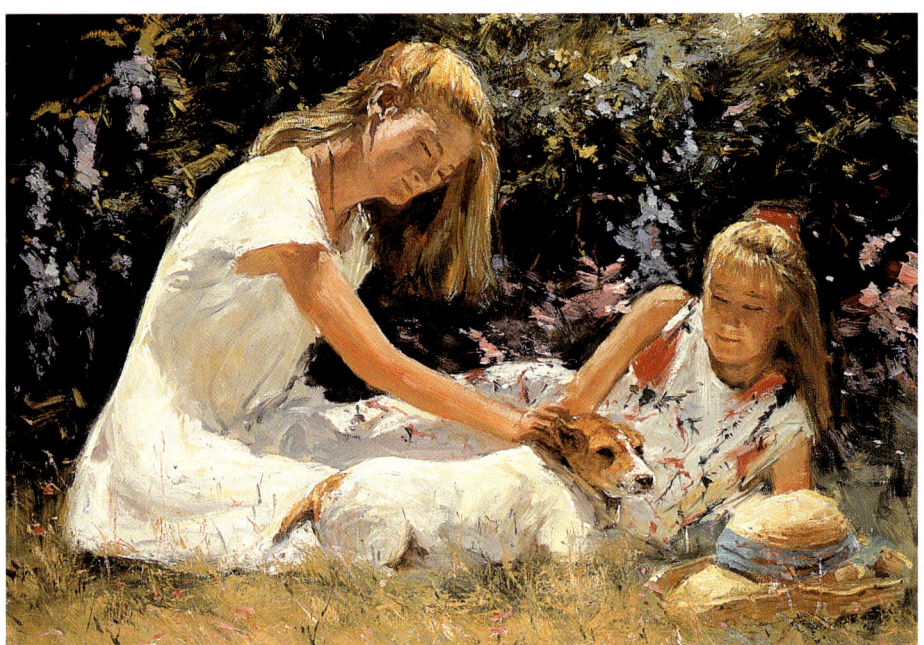

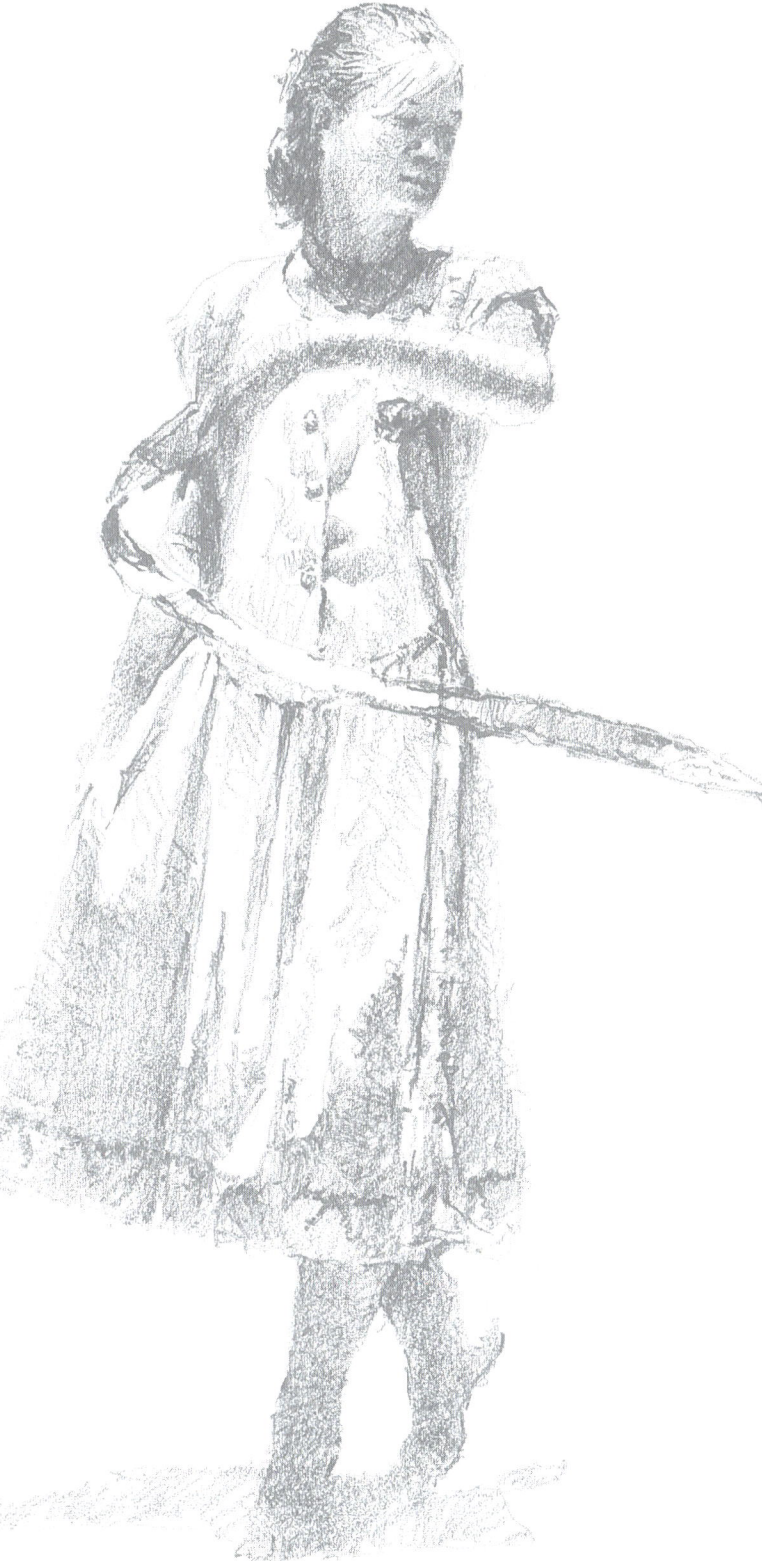

> Recollect that the Almighty, who gave
> The dog to be companion of our
> pleasures and our toils
> Hath invested him with a nature noble
> And incapable of deceit.
>
> — SIR WALTER SCOTT
> (1771–1832)

My friends Mike and Liz assured me that that's exactly what happened, so it must be true. The happy ending to this story is that little Rusty is now a permanent resident at the home of Mike and Liz and their two lovely young daughters.

But how did little Rusty manage the twenty-mile trip? Blowed if I know, but I guess the little fella knew he had a warm, loving home waiting for him if only he could find it. I guess that's what kept him going. He's a true Jack Russell in that respect…he never gave up.

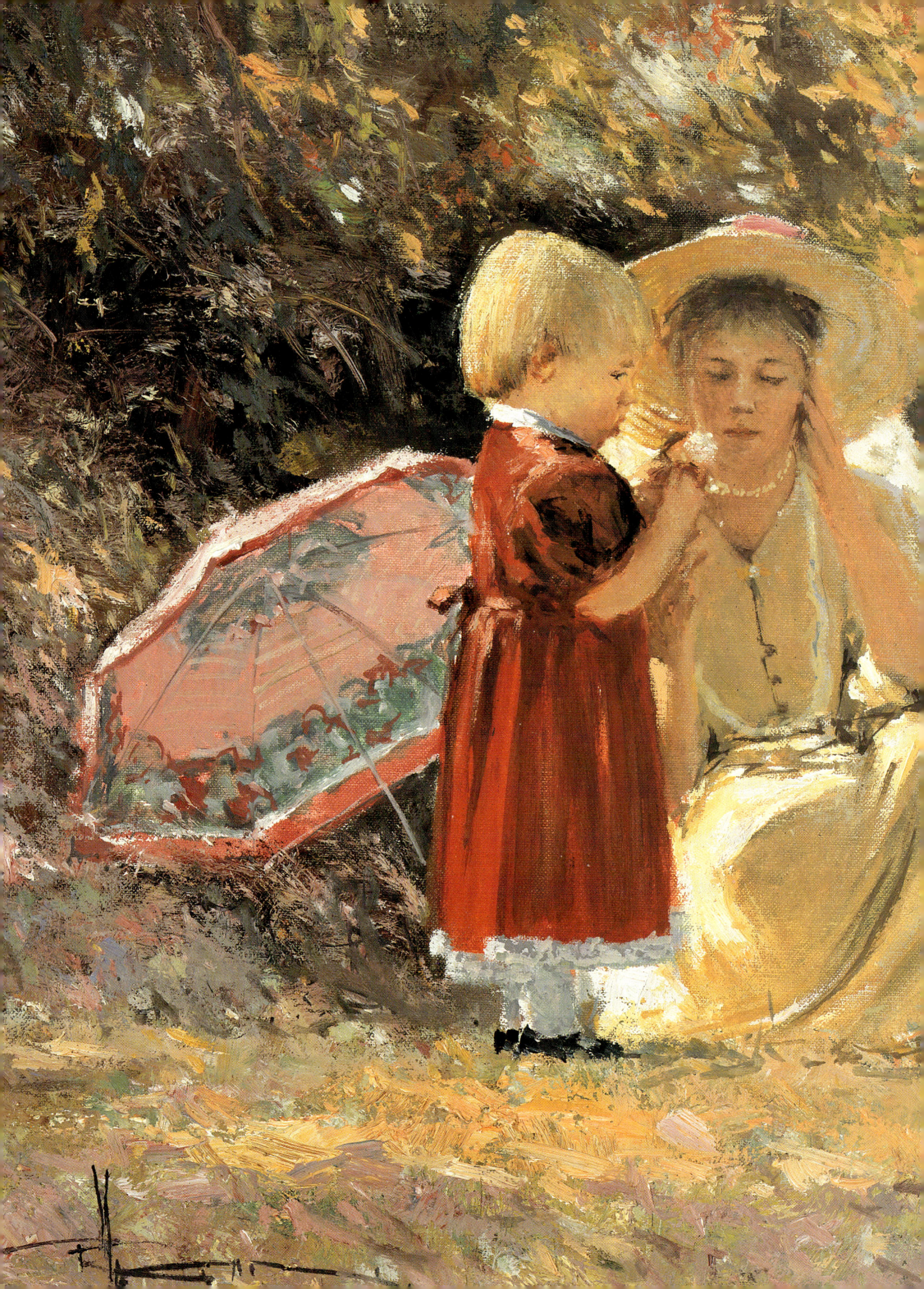

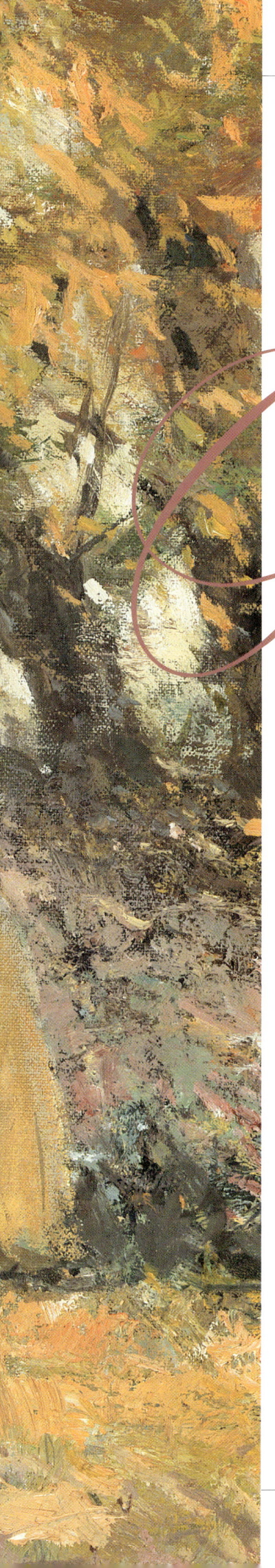

Rosie's Dandelions

Dandelions, according to Mr. Webster's dictionary, are "common plants, abundant in meadows and gardens, with widely toothed leaves. A dandelion clock is the head of the parachute-like fruit on the plant and children make believe they can tell time by blowing away the fruits."

So much for Mr. Webster, but now meet a real expert on dandelions. This is Rosie, aged two years and nine months and looking very pretty in her scarlet dress as she blows on dandelions with just a little help from her big sister. Rosie is an absolute whiz at blowing on dandelions and then guessing the correct time within about an eleven-hour margin.

Growing Up

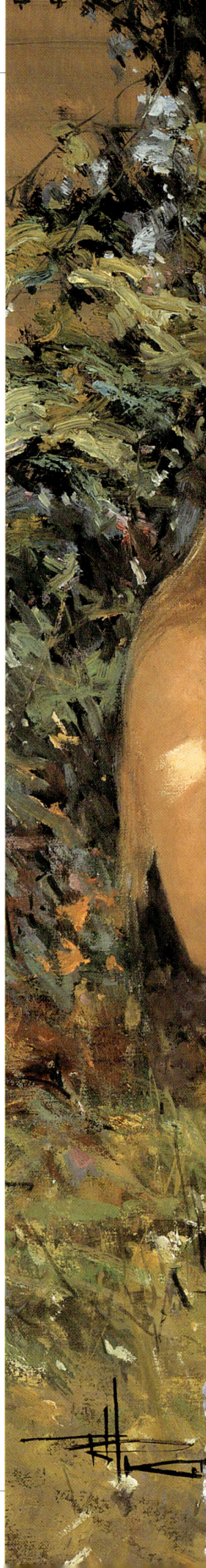

If my memory serves me correctly, it was the comedy genius, Danny Kaye, surprisingly enough, who recorded a very thought-provoking song back in the early 1960s about the rapid passing of time. It concerned, essentially, how time passes from a father's point of view as he incredulously watches his daughter growing to young womanhood…the years flying by so fast he barely realizes what is happening. How very true this is.

"Don't come in!" I seem to remember were the strident key words in the lyrics of this wonderfully intuitive old song. It was that simple declaration that so succinctly described how the daughter had reached the age where she was suddenly demanding her independence and privacy. Seemingly, it was just an eye blink ago that she was a helpless babe in arms. But another eye blink later the father knocks on her door and that's when she shouts back in her startled alarm, "Don't come in!"

It was at that stopping-him-dead-in-his-tracks moment when he realized his little girl was most definitely growing up.

For some parents this particular moment of enlightenment can strike much earlier, providing we are observant enough to heed the telltale signals.

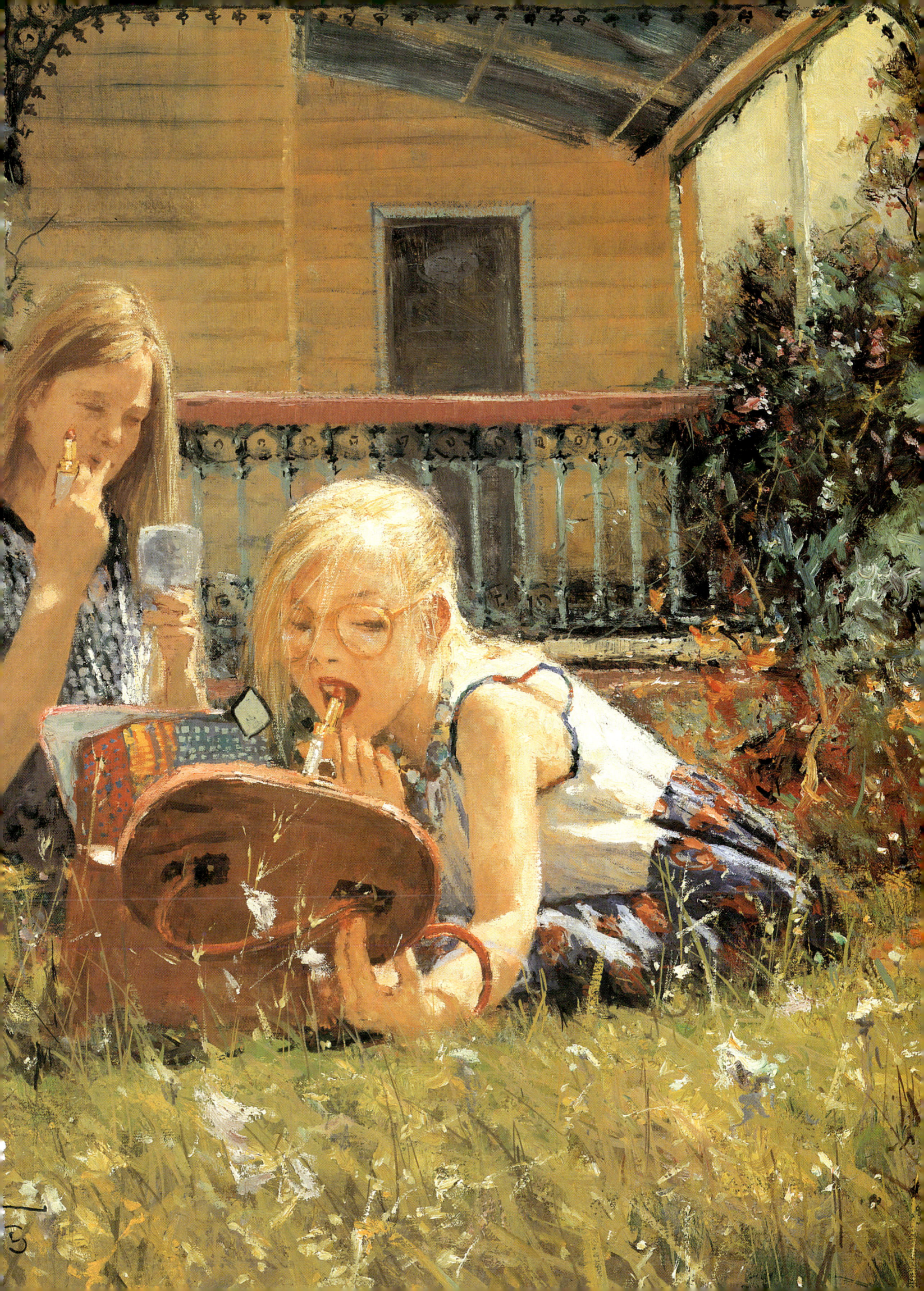

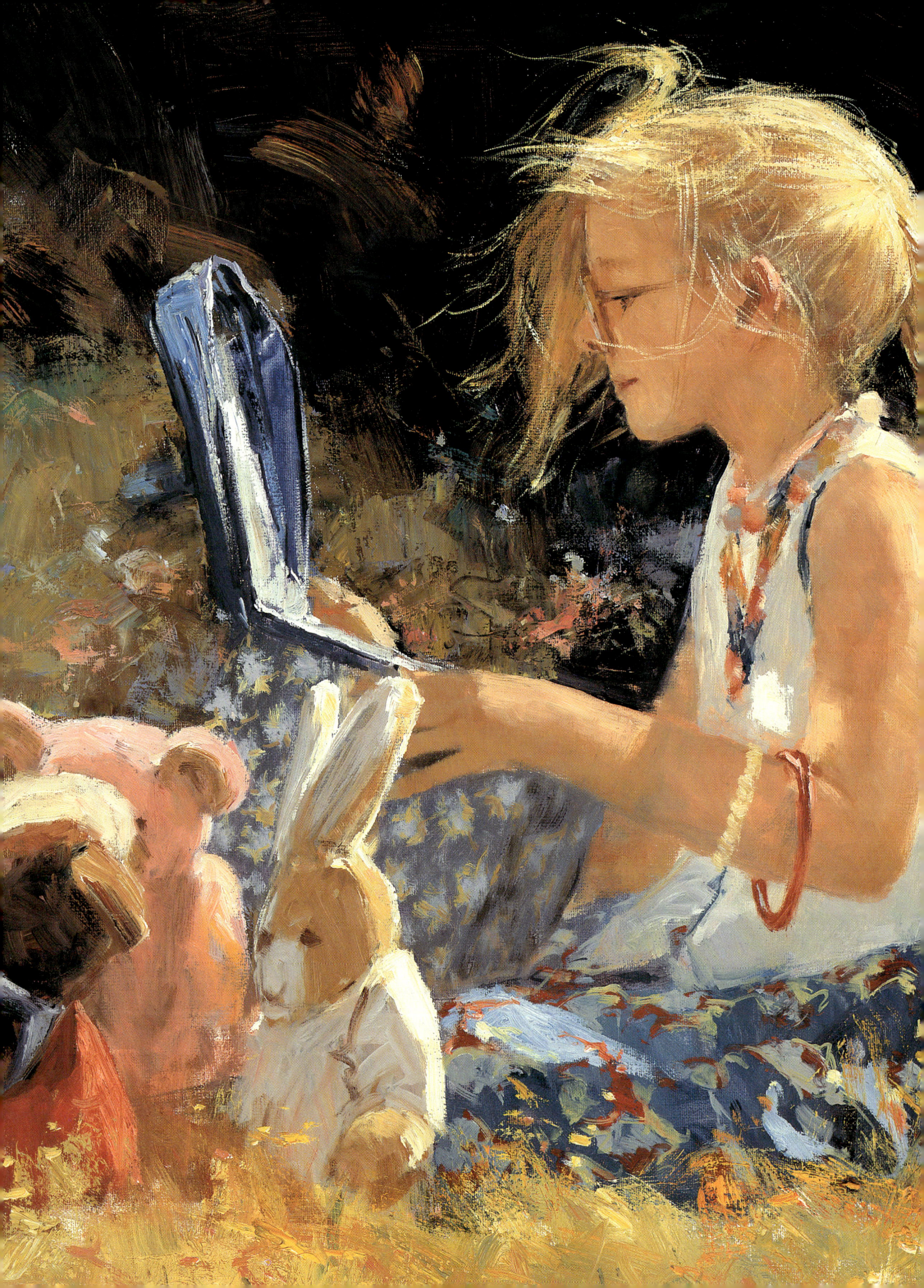

When she's about six or seven, perhaps even younger, the first usually comical signs begin to appear. She will probably find one of Mommy's old straw hats and a pair of high-heeled shoes that are about six sizes too big. With them on she'll go clicketty-clacketting all the way down the front pathway until she trips and has to pull herself up again, with as much dignity as she can muster.

A few years later, when she's around ten or eleven, but it often happens even earlier of course, she and her freckled-face girlfriend from around the corner will furtively sneak a couple of tubes of Mommy's lipstick, a powder puff and a mirror. And now they're really ready for the big time.

Outside the house they scurry and hide behind a tree and then, with much stifled giggling, and many darting looks all around to check that no one is watching, so begins their first makeover.

The next big step after that is trying on their training bras in the privacy of their rooms. And at this point, if you happen to knock on the door and hear the shrieking command: "Don't come in!" – Then, Dad, that's your day of dawning. The day when you're supposed to realize once and for all that your little girl is not so little anymore. She's growing up.

It's a painful realization for poor old Dad, and he never really faces up to it, because no matter how many years pass by, she'll always be Daddy's little girl to him. There's an old saying that just about sums it up: "A little girl's first love affair is with her father. After a while she gets over it. But the father never does."

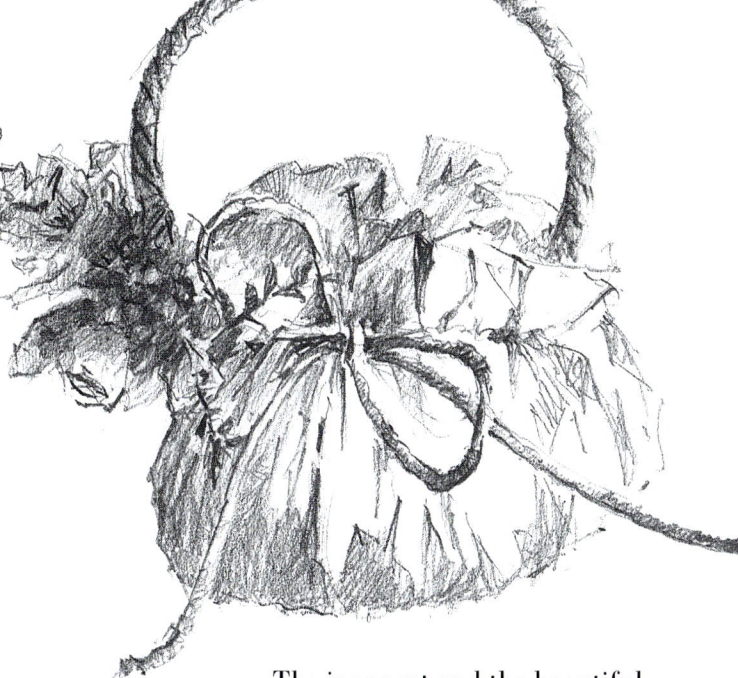

**The innocent and the beautiful
Have no enemy but time.**

— WILLIAM BUTLER YEATS
(1865–1939)

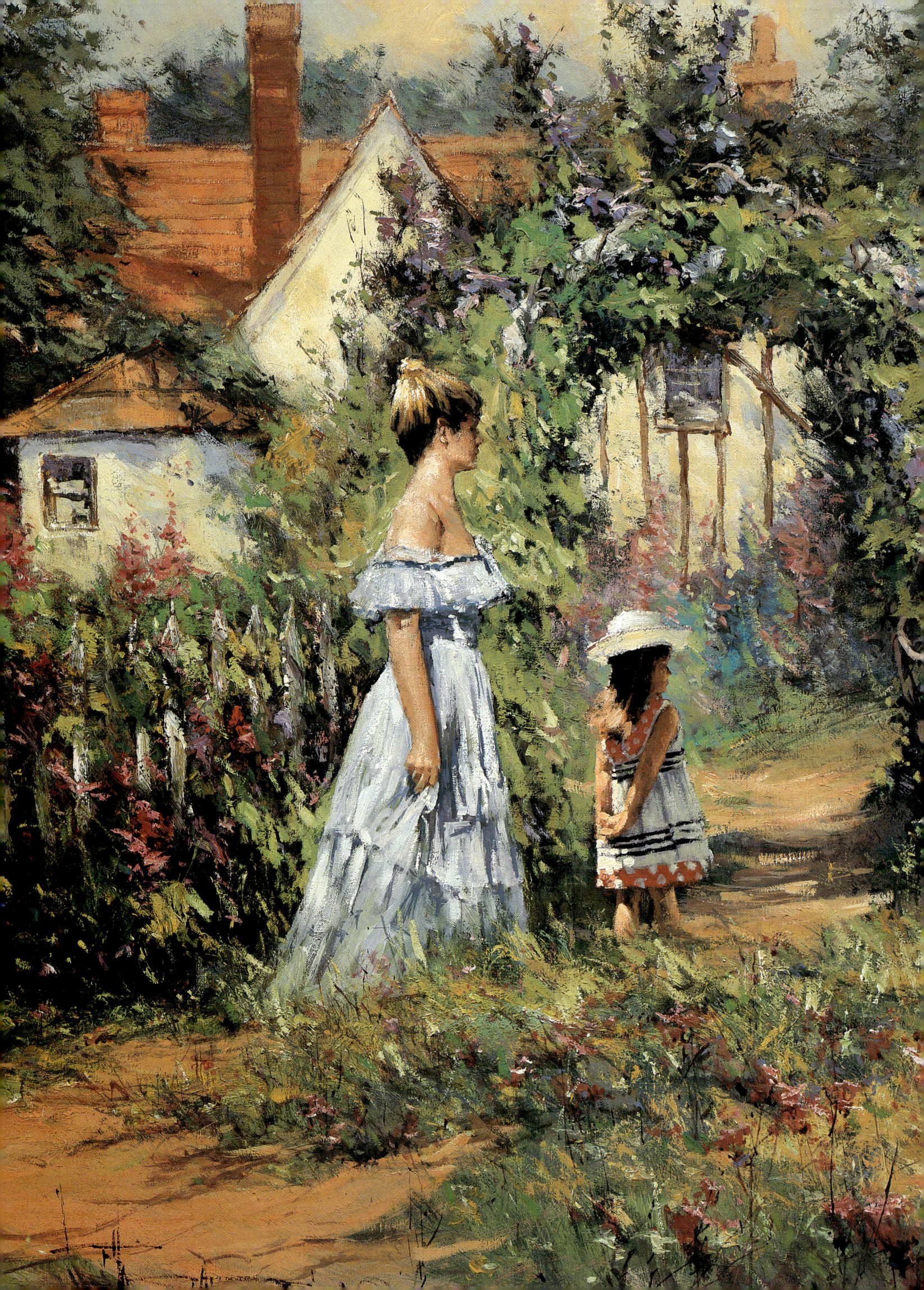

"I know a little garden close
Set thick with lily and red rose
Where I would wander if I might
From early morn to dewy night."

— WILLIAM MORRIS
(1834–1895)

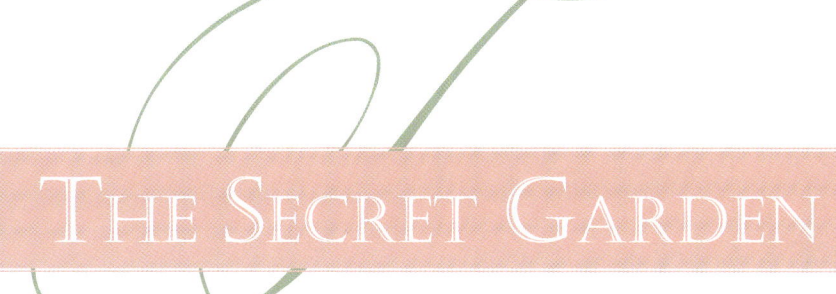

THE SECRET GARDEN

In her secret garden she strolls so slowly, so thoughtfully among the endless variety of gently swaying blooms.

She calls it her secret garden because it is known only to herself. It exists only in her mind, in her recurring dream. Here she can roam and relax in a fragrant, romantic refuge from the world's unrelenting sadness. All of those problems are on the outside, far beyond her protective petalled walls. Here in her secret garden, full of hyacinths, azaleas, roses and lilies…there is no reason for sadness, nor even a reason to feel lonely.

Here she is happily surrounded by many, many friends. And they are all flowers.

*"The human heart
has secret treasures
In secret kept
In silence sealed."*

— CHARLOTTE
BRONTE
(1816–1855)

"Every daisy in the dell
Knows my secret
Knows it well
And yet I dare not tell."

To Kiss That Little Face

She was sitting next to me on a long, seemingly endless flight from New York to the West Coast and we'd never met before, but you know how it is on a really long flight – even strangers eventually get to talking.

She had genuinely golden hair, the kindest blue eyes and was very attractive in a quiet, unpretentious way. I guess, she was probably in her early 30s. At first she seemed rather shy and reserved, but when the steward brought the coffee around she began to relax, and we gradually started talking about, well, nothing much in particular.

She told me she had been in New York City for the last six weeks, much longer than she planned, and was eagerly looking forward to returning home to her three-year-old daughter.

I informed her that I also had a daughter, admittedly a few years older than her little one. So, sure enough, as every proud parent would do in this coincidental situation, we both immediately dived for our picture wallets. I must have seen more John Wayne movies than the lady next to me because I easily outdrew her, and while she was fumbling in her purse, I'd already flashed the photograph of my own button-nosed Little Miss Bossyboots in front of her.

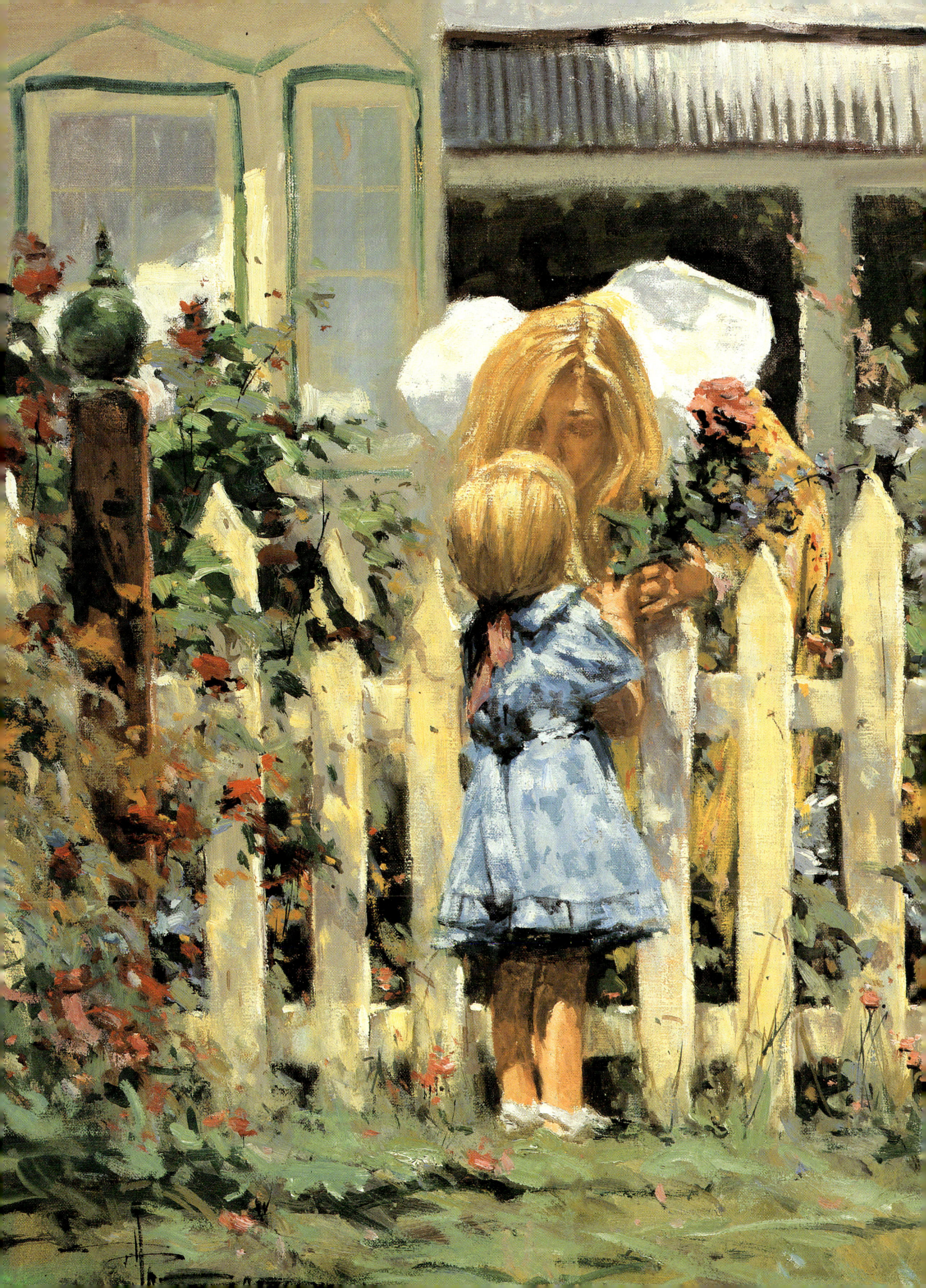

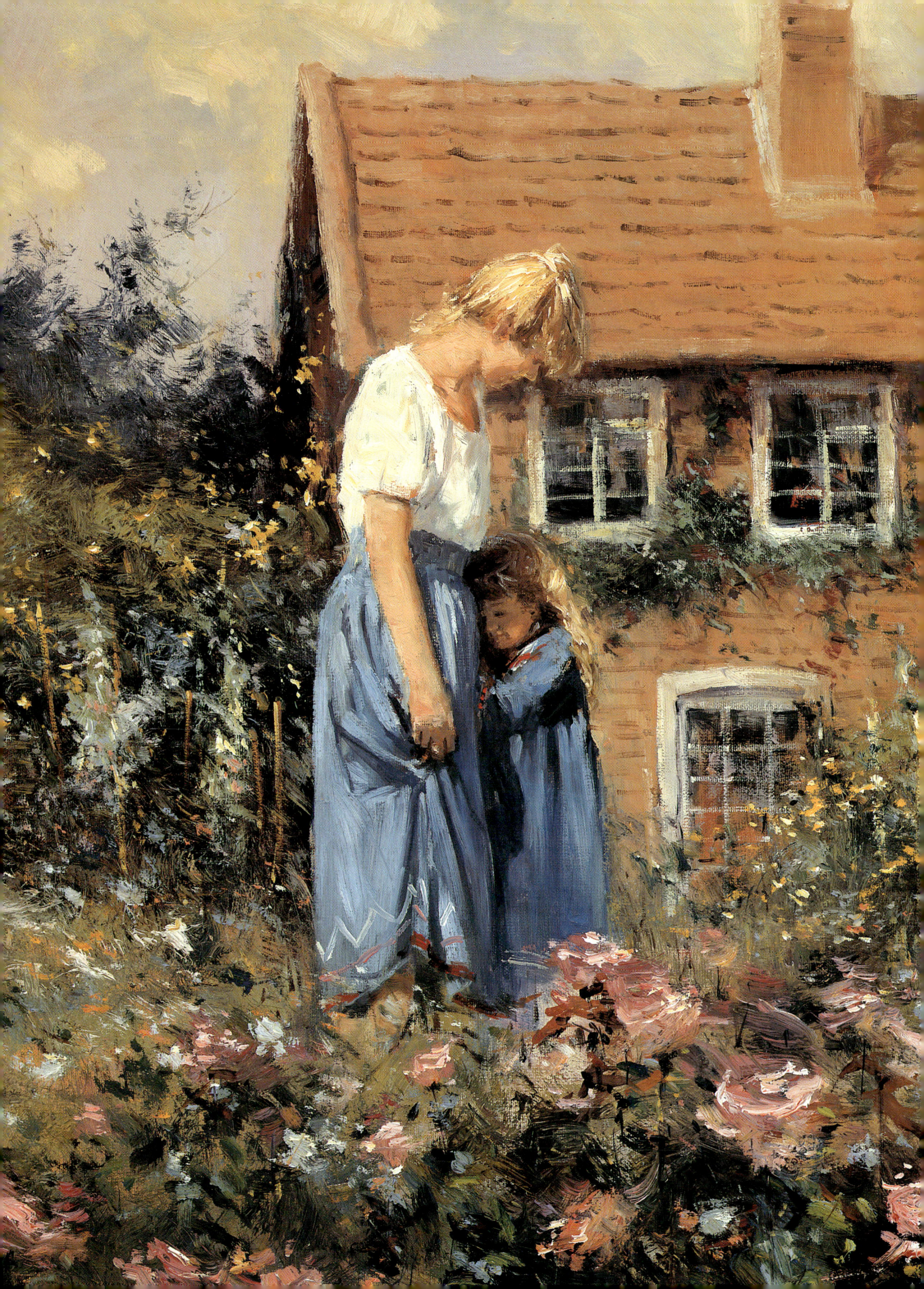

*There is a garden in her face
Where roses and white lilies grow
A heavenly paradise is that place
Wherein all pleasant fruits do flow.*

– THOMAS CAMPION
(1567–1620)

The lady duly showed me the photo of her own child, and I had to concede that, regardless of my bias toward my own children, this little girl of hers had the most beautiful, angelic face I had ever seen. I handed the photo back and the lady then stared at it herself, in complete silence, for a surprisingly long time – at least a couple of minutes.

Then, with the tears welling up in her eyes, she said in a trembling, emotional voice, "After six long weeks, you can't imagine how much I'm aching to get back home and kiss that little face again."

I smiled and nodded agreement, but for a moment or two I didn't quite understand. And then her beautiful words suddenly translated into a clear picture in my head – a very private, very personal image. I saw myself walking in the door of a house I'd been away from for far too long. I saw my own daughter rushing down the hallway to greet me. She jumped into my arms and…yes, I kissed that little face I love so dearly.

The sweet embrace of a loving child…Aren't we foolish the way we take such treasured moments so much for granted?

Her angel's face
As the great eye of heaven shined bright
And made a sunshine in the shady place.

— EDMUND SPENCER
(1552-1599)

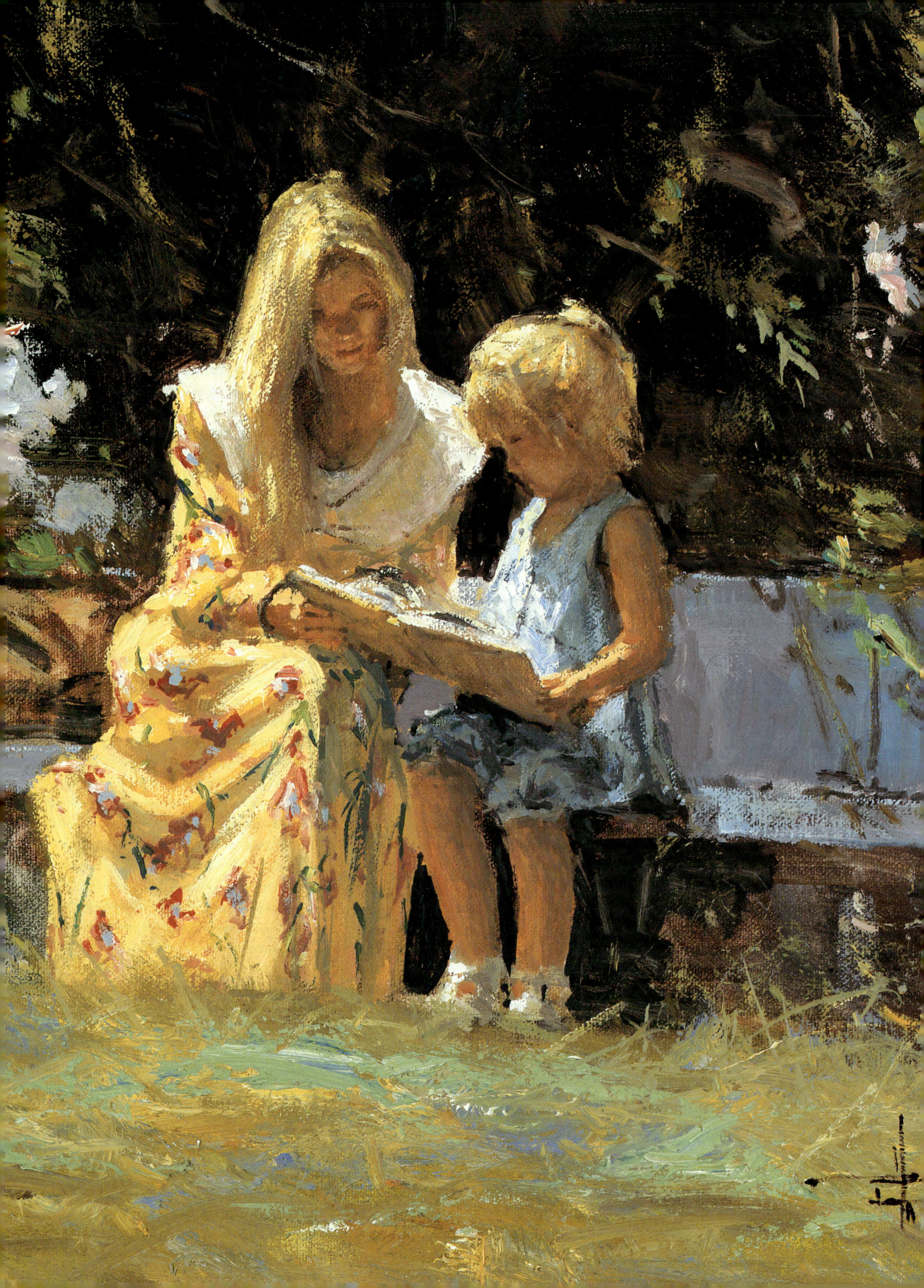

It's Storytime

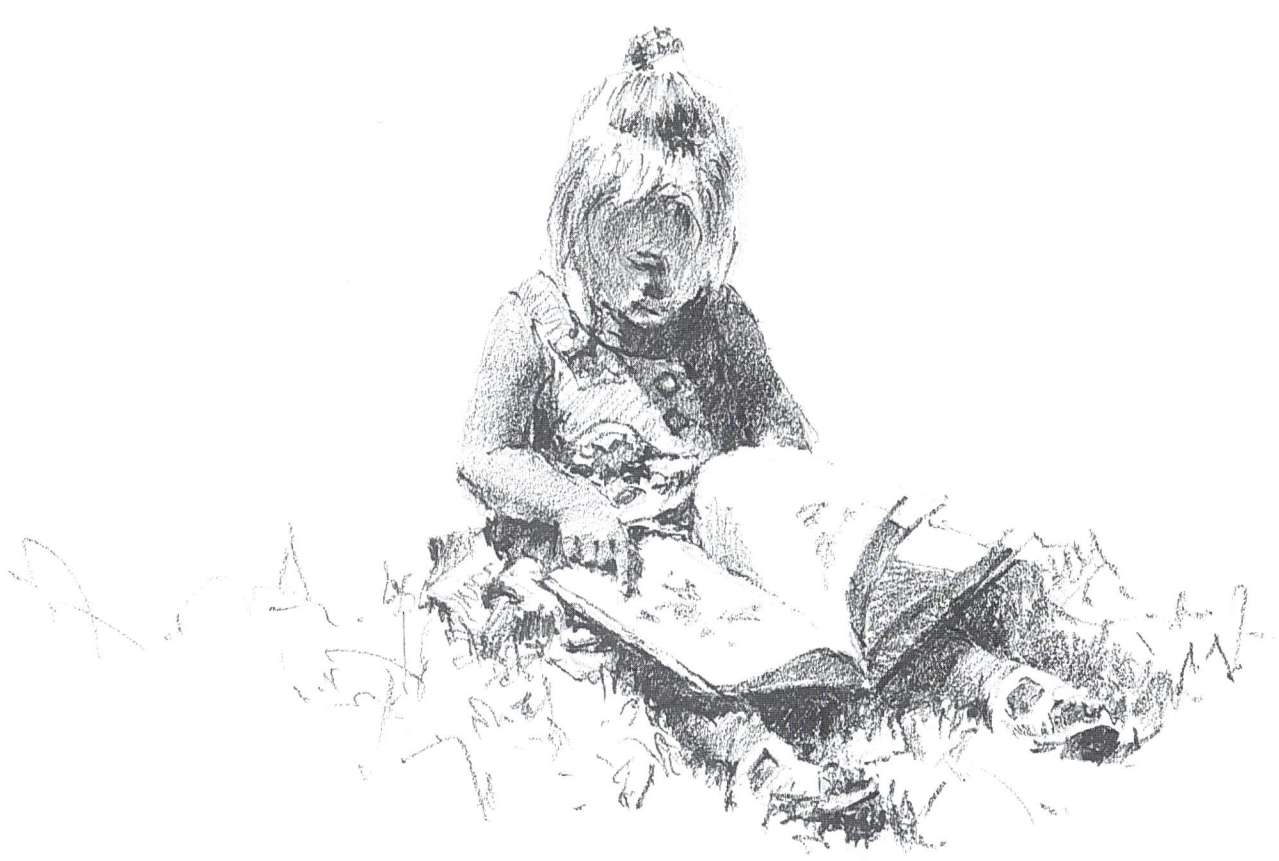

She was sitting on the garden bench and reading a fairy story to her little one. The morning sunlight was dancing on their golden hair. It was such a deeply private, bonding moment between them…that not even a butterfly would dare disturb.

June Bridesmaid

She was nineteen and was dressed in a bridesmaid gown because her big sister, five years older, was getting married on this beautiful spring morning.

A June bride and a June bridesmaid, and all in the family. How perfectly natural it all seemed with everything unfolding in its proper chronological order. The white limousines will be arriving in a few minutes time to take the bride, the bride's father and the bride's sister to the church. Inside the house there is the usual last minute panic as the bride takes a look at herself in the full-length mirror and worries if she will manage to walk down the aisle without tripping over her train.

Today, the bride is center of all attention, the cynosure of all eyes, the star of the show. So the young bridesmaid slips away, unnoticed for a stroll in the back garden. Just to be by herself for a few moments, with her own private thoughts about her own uncertain future.

She is simultaneously happy and sad — happy for her sister and sad for herself because she is losing her inspiration, the role model she has always looked up to. Things will never be the same again.

"Why did she want to get married?" She asks herself. "I don't, I don't ever want to get married — not ever, not ever, not ever!"

But this is all part of the growing up process, and deep down she knows she doesn't really mean it.

Without admitting it to herself she knows that on one day, one sunny spring day, just like this, her turn will come. So don't be at all surprised, if after her sister's wedding, outside the church, when it comes time for the bride to toss away the bouquet…the little sister bridesmaid will leap like a gazelle to catch it. No one will leap higher.

"The year's at the spring
And day's at the morn
Morning's at seven
The hillside's dew-pear led
The lark's on the wing
The snail's on the thorn
God's in his heaven -
All's right with the world."

— ROBERT BROWNING

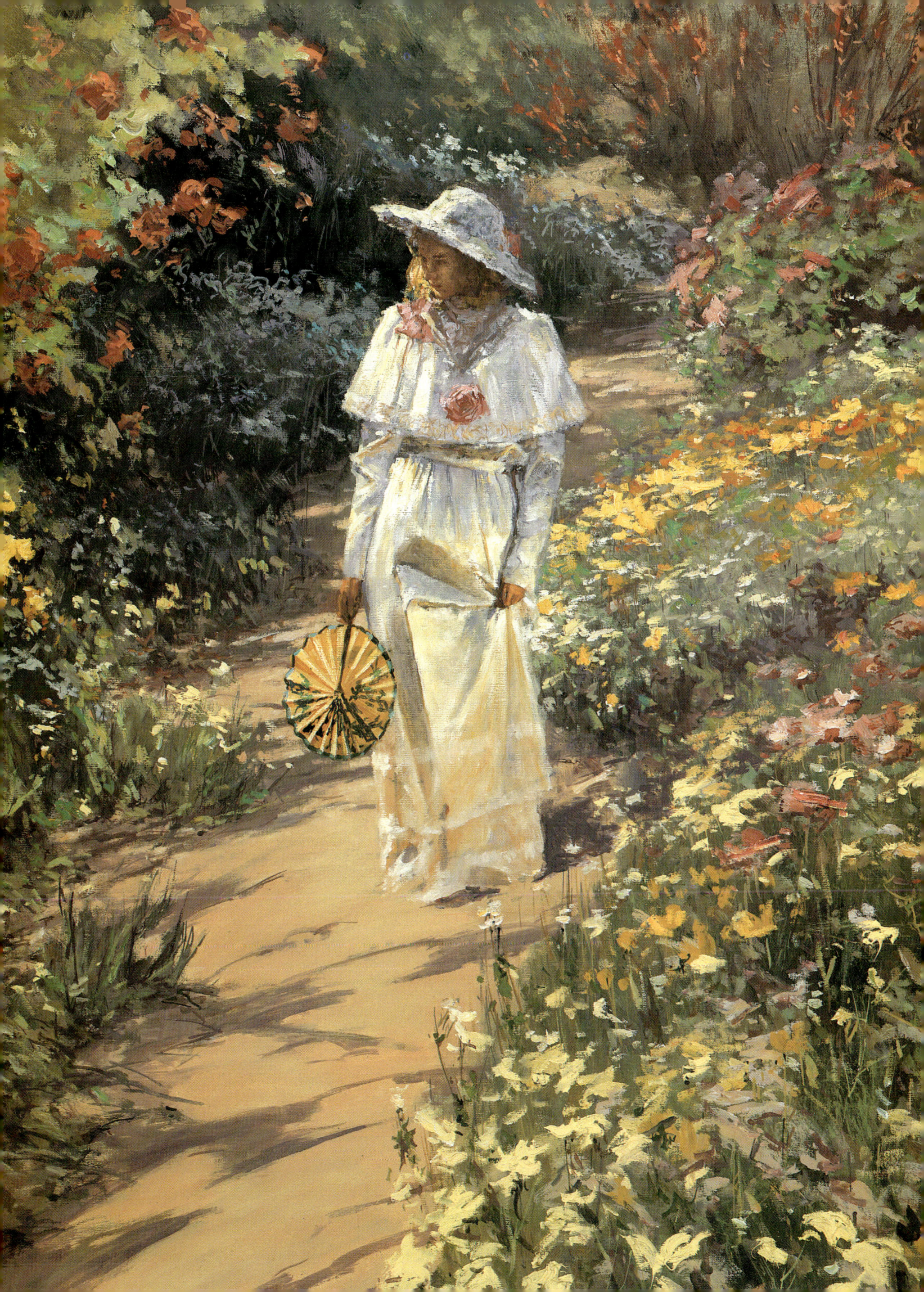

Her First Beau

There's Melanie out there in the back garden of her Californian family home – right next door to my place. She's just turned four years old and you won't believe what she's up to now. She's gone and put on her best party dress and she's pirouetting in front of Little Beau – to impress him.

Little Beau, who's also just turned four, doesn't know it yet, but whether he likes the idea or not, Melanie has decided to grant him the unique honor of becoming her first boyfriend. California girls sure snap 'em up early, don't they?

Just thinking about Melanie and Little Beau, it occurs to me that there is a fashionable theory nowadays that little boys and girls behave as differently as they do only because of conditioning from birth. But, having three kids of my own and enough nephews and nieces to seriously affect Disneyland's annual profits, I just can't buy that idea at all. From my personal observations, I have no doubts whatsoever that little girls will be little girls and little boys will be little boys and that's the way it is, was and always will be.

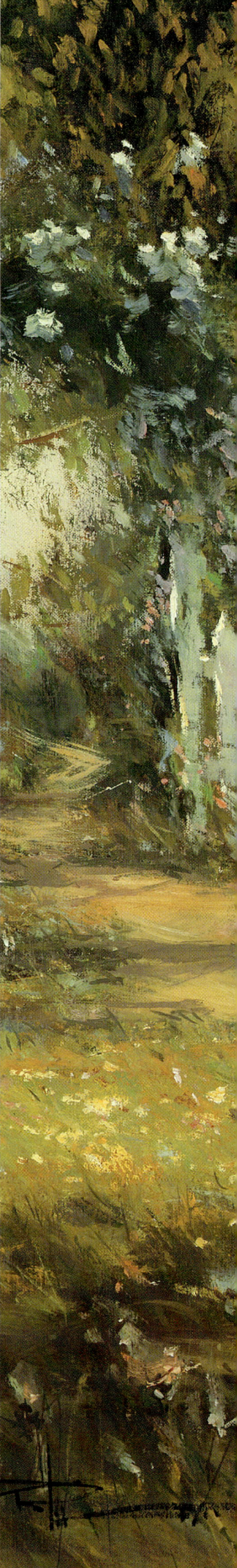

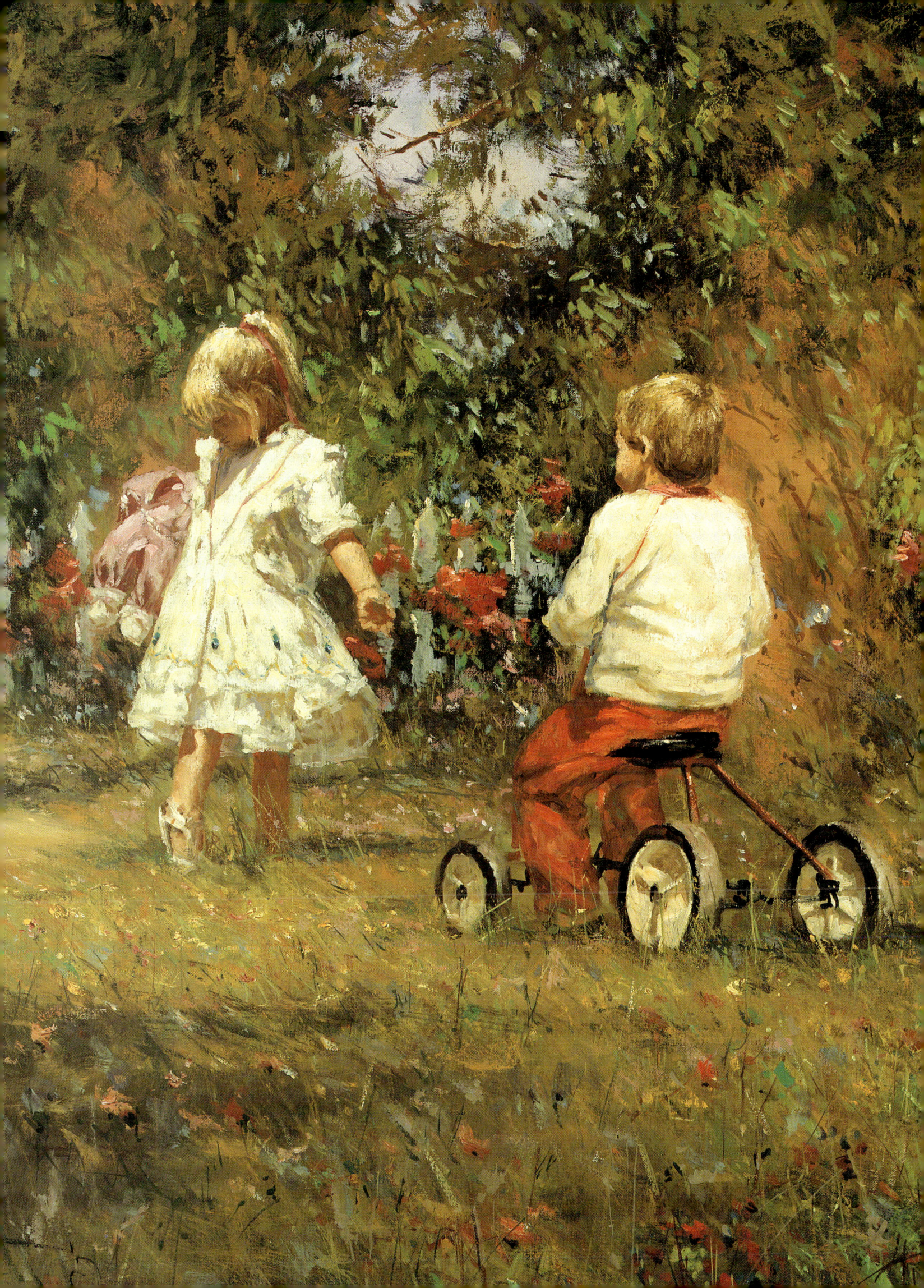

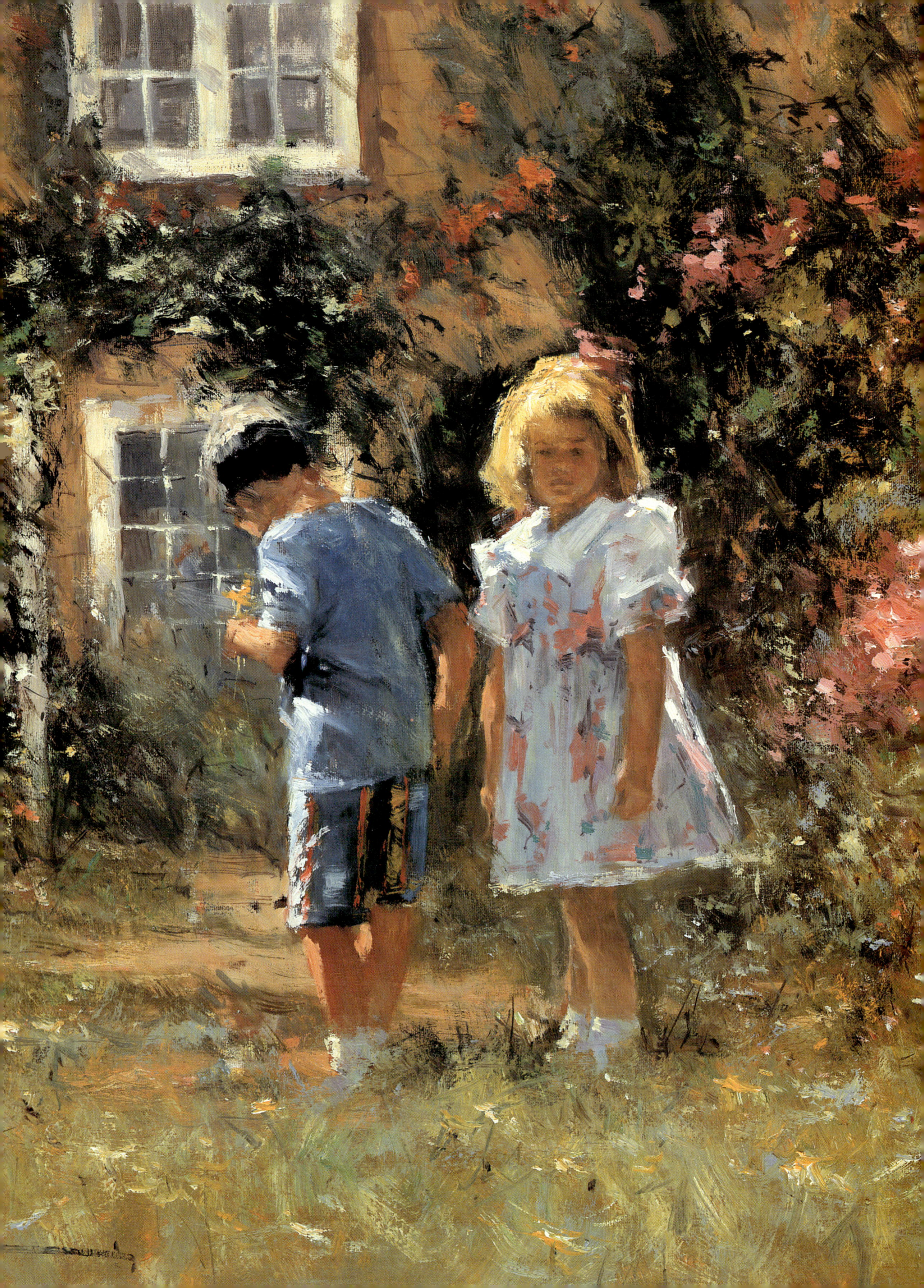

In a relationship between a little boy and little girl you must have noticed that it is always the little girl who makes the first move. She starts looking for a boyfriend at about five, after she's learned to walk, and the poor unfortunate little guy she's set her cap for can't do much about it. All he really can do is hop on his tricycle and make his getaway as fast as his little feet can peddle. At any rate, that's what invariably happens whenever Melanie decides she wants to give Beau a cuddle.

One day Little Beau pedaled up to me on his little three-wheeler kiddybike and he looked so miserable I was quite concerned. So I said, "Hey Beau, what's the long face for, buddy? Did you fall off your bike?" And Little Beau looked up at me with the saddest tear-stained face I've ever seen and said, "Melanie keeps kissing me!" And then the poor little guy just burst into tears.

There's no doubt about it, life sure is tough for a four-year-old little boy when a four-year-old little girl has a colossal crush on him.

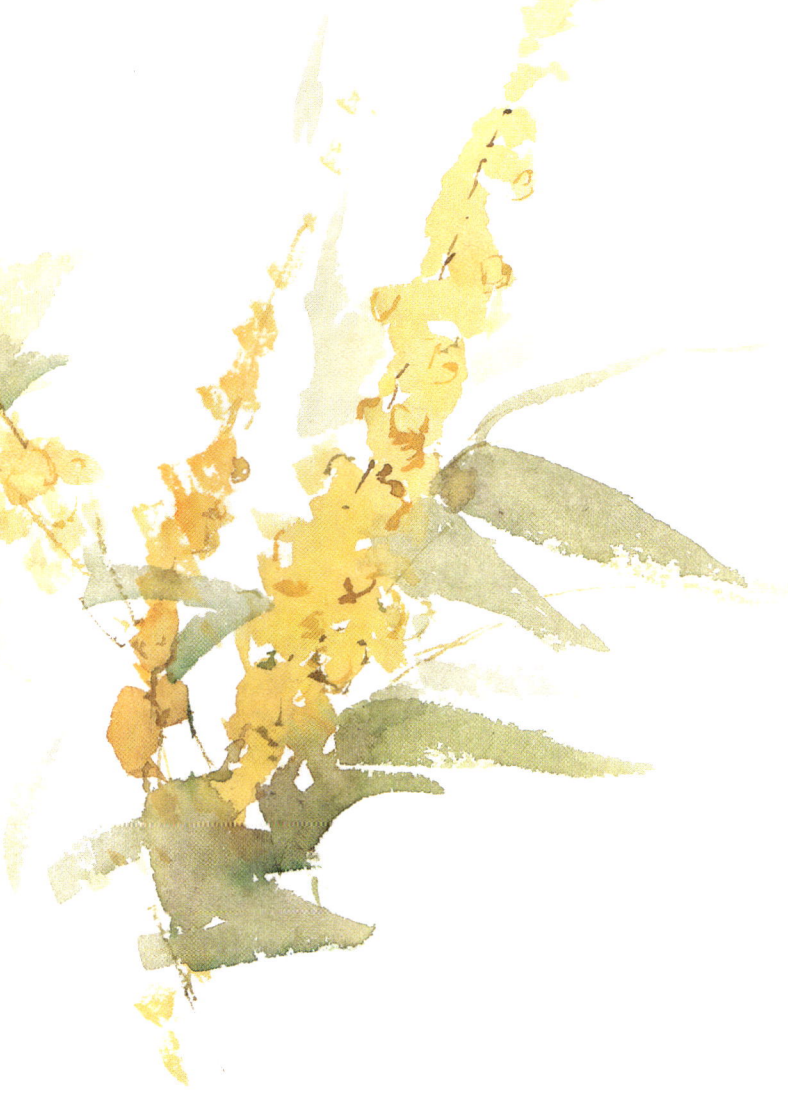

Wahine

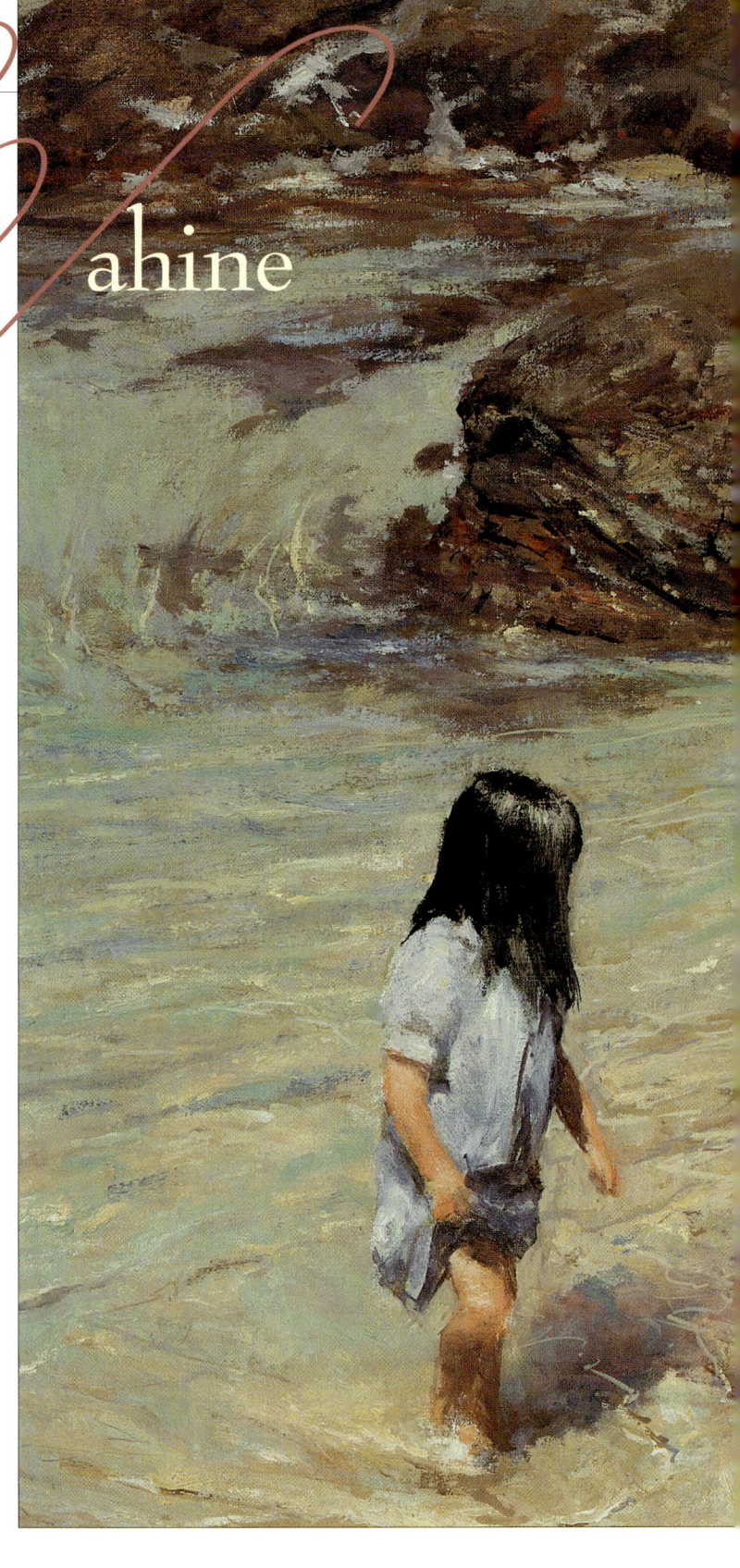

For most tourists who have journeyed to the enchanting islands of Hawaii, the only downside aspect of their visit comes at the very end – the inevitably melancholy moment of departure.

To arrive in Hawaii is a joy, but to depart is to be filled with saddening thoughts that perhaps you may never have the chance to return.

I have been lucky enough to have made the trip far across the Pacific to Hawaii many times and enjoyed every moment of my carefree wanderings through this unique tropical paradise. It is a wrench to have to leave, and I am always overcome by a profound feeling of regretfulness whenever the time comes to board the plane and return to life's relentless realities. As the plane taxies down the runway, I'm invariably overcome by a dark foreboding that circumstances could prevent me from ever coming back to heavenly Hawaii. This is enough to bring a lump in the throat and even tears to the eyes.

Sometimes, on these meditative farewell occasions, I recall that haunting final scene from one of my all-time favorite motion pictures, "From Here To Eternity." It was a film made in Hawaii in the early 1950s and nowadays it only turns up on TV in the early hours of the morning. Even though it was made so many years ago, those final moments in the movie will never be out of date.

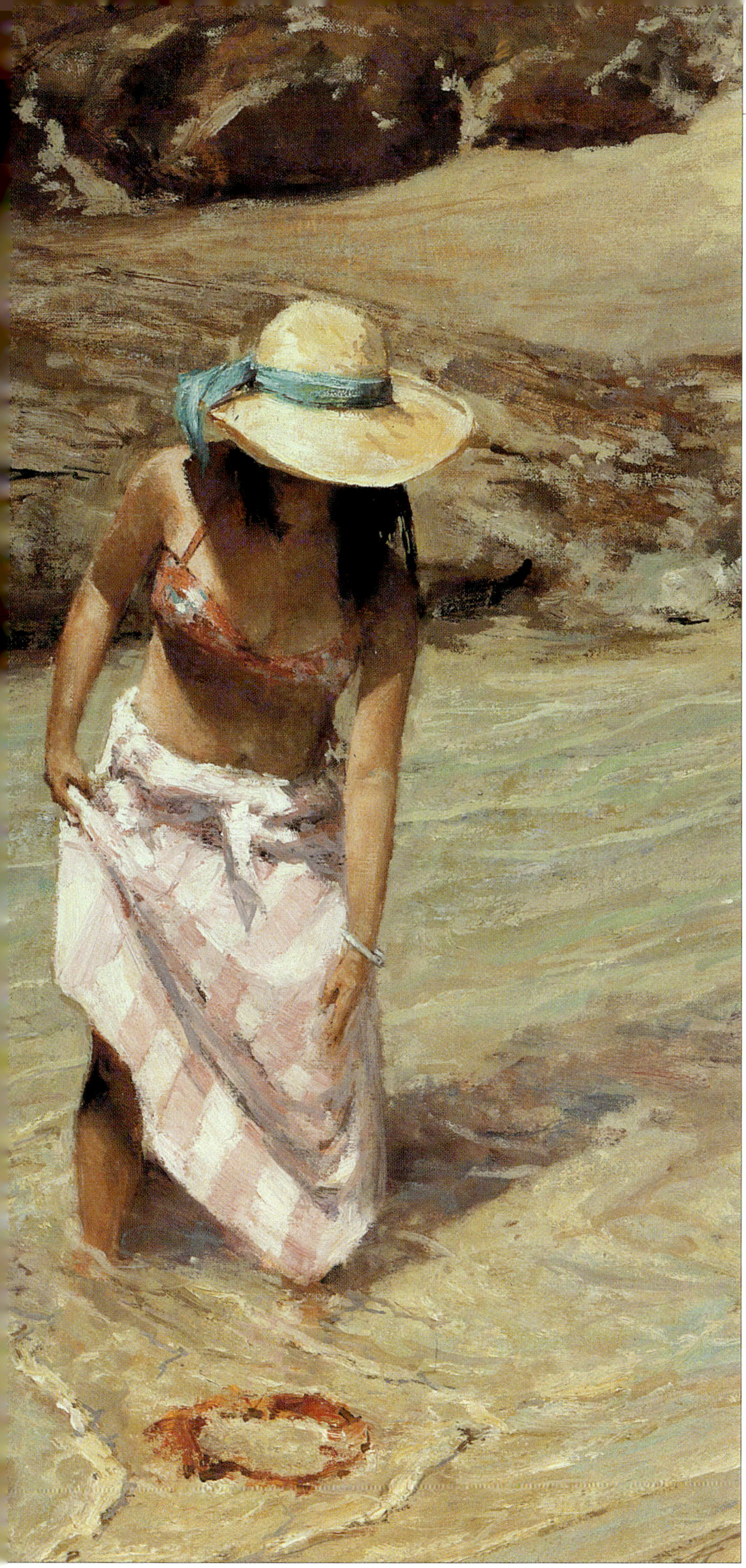

someday return, but if the lei floats out to sea then you will never come back. Did their leis return?

The film left the question unanswered and yet, sadly, we somehow knew the ladies would not be returning to the once-innocent Hawaii that war had changed forever.

That tradition of the leis is widely believed to be traced to a practice of passengers tossing leis overboard as they departed Hawaii in sailing ships in the late 19th century. But on my last Hawaiian visit I heard of an even more romantic version of that tradition that goes back possibly hundreds of years.

I was told that when a young wahine had lost her lover she would stand on the edge of a deserted beach and toss a garland of flowers into the surging waves. If the lei came back, he would someday return to her. But if the flowers floated out to sea, her lover was gone forever.

It is such a lovely and truly romantic tradition, that in picturing it in my mind, I think I prefer a happy ending. Perhaps old King Neptune, the God of the Sea, will take pity on the beautiful wahine and turn the tide around…and send the flowers and, symbolically, her lost lover, rushing back to her waiting arms.

The scene showed the two female leads, Deborah Kerr and Donna Reed, as civilian women reluctantly leaving Honolulu after the invasion of Pearl Harbor. As their ship pulled away from the pier, they threw their garlands of flowers (their leis) into the sea. According to an Hawaiian tradition, if your lei floats back to the island you will

Gone A Wandering

There comes a time in a young girl's life, usually in her early teens, when she quietly develops the habit of wandering off somewhere, all by herself. She doesn't go far, but she just wants to be alone, completely alone – if only for a few minutes.

That is a fairly broad generalization, of course, and not all young girls have this occasional solitude-seeking inclination. But it happens often enough to be a part of family life that most parents of young girls will be familiar with. "Where has Louise disappeared to now?" inquires the exasperated father at the Thanksgiving family picnic outing. "I'm just about ready to carve the turkey."

"Oh, she's all right, let her be," the ever-understanding mother reassures. "She's just gone a' wandering off amongst the trees. She'll be back in a couple of minutes or so."

And perhaps just fifty yards away, but out of sight and beyond the hearing of the family chatter, Louise is idly strolling through the forest, smiling at the birds overhead, smelling the flowers – communing with nature in a daydream world all her own.

She seeks a secret place like this to ponder her uncertain future, to think about the great changes that will soon be taking place in her life once she leaves school. Will she go on to college? Will she travel to distant lands? Will she find someone and fall in love? Her impatient young mind is both wandering and wondering. This is her personal pause in her day's occupations. For a few blissfully, peaceful and intensely private moments, she is far away from life's mundane realities.

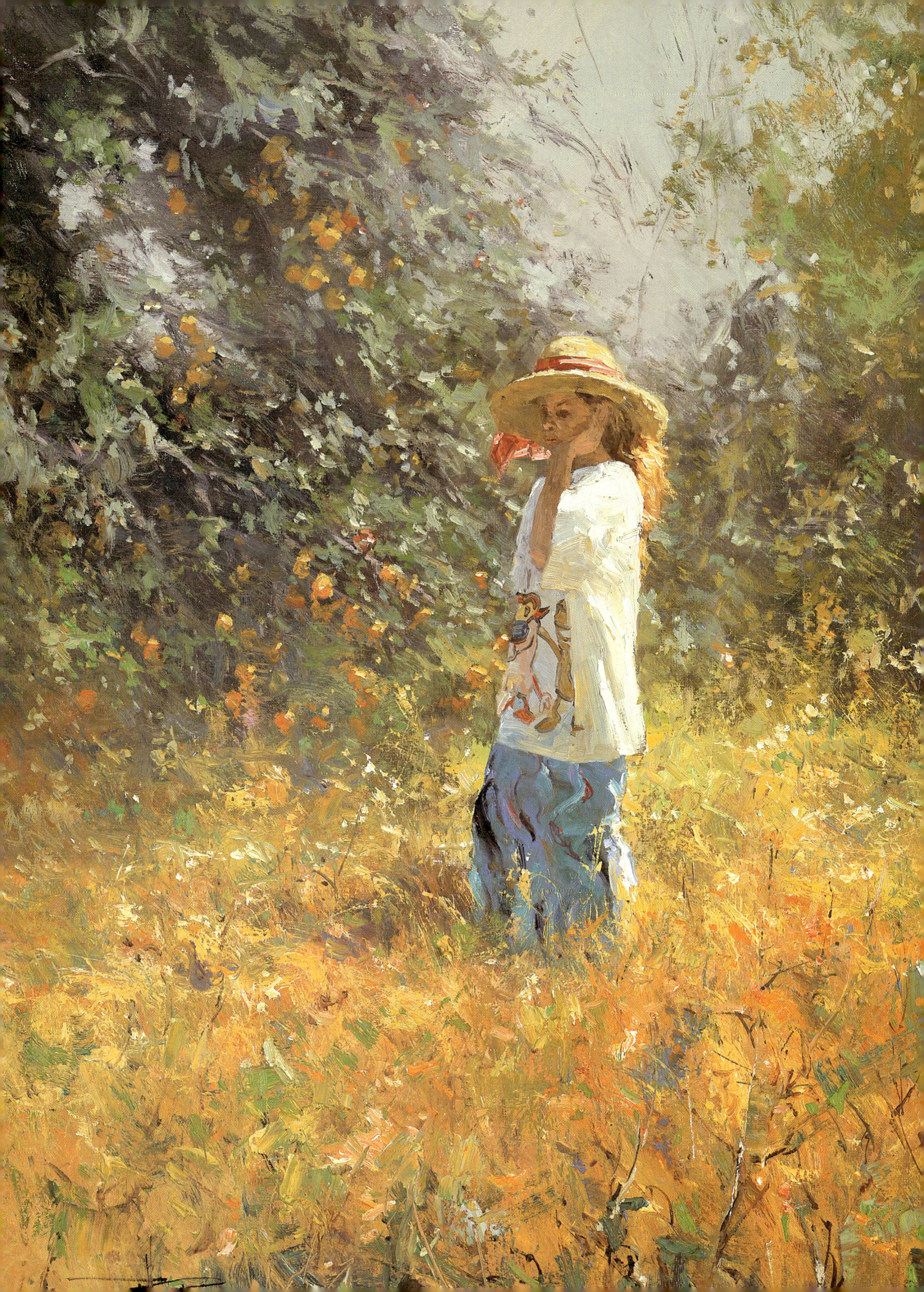

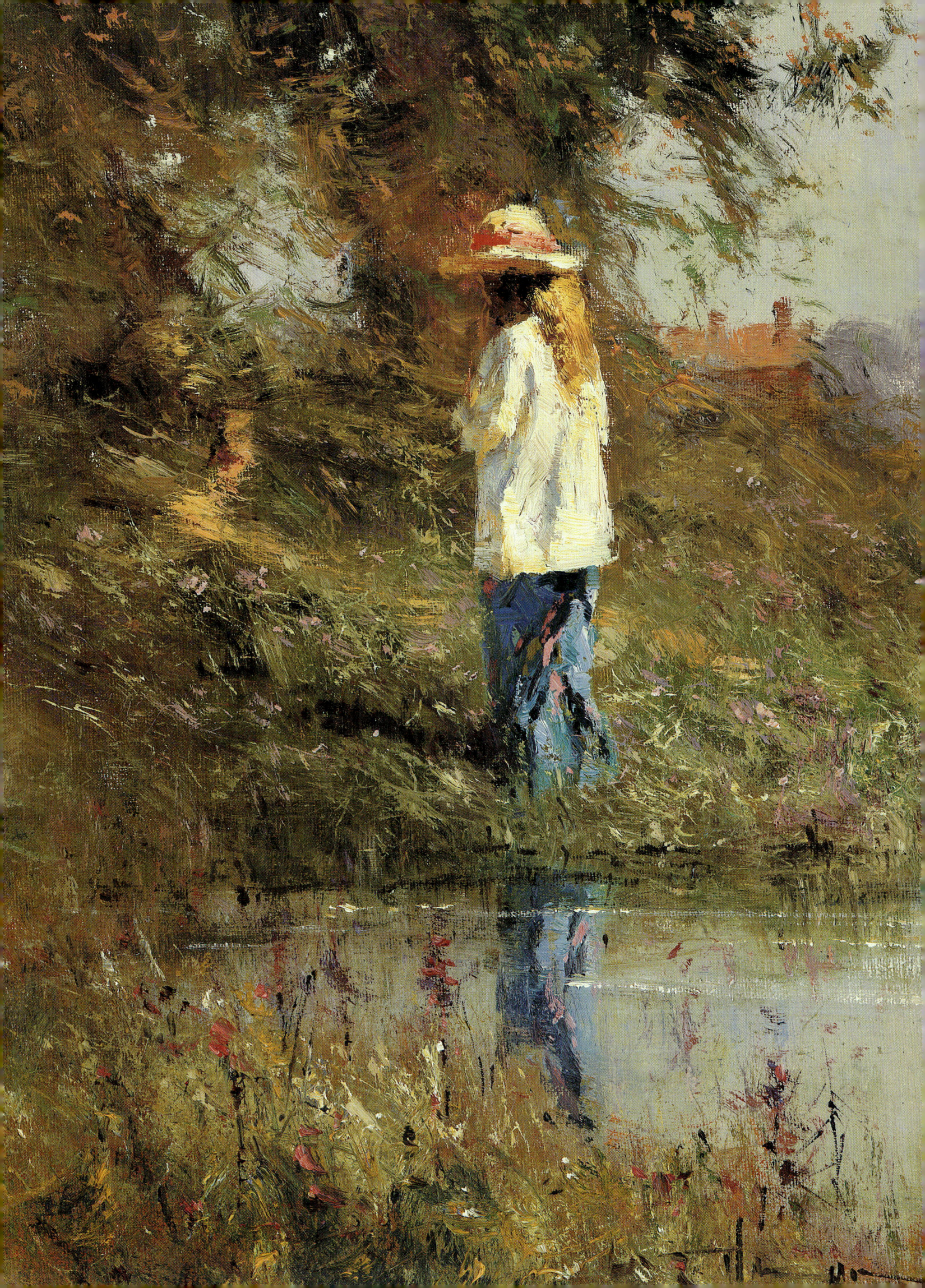

*"Thanks to the human heart
By which we live
Thanks to the tenderness
It's joys and fears
To me the meanest flower that blows
Can give
Thoughts that do often lie too deep
For tears."*

—WILLIAM WORDSWORTH
(1770–1850)

Sometimes, when all her little problems seem to be piling up, there is a very real need for her to just wander away like this…softly and unnoticed, just to be able to think things out all by herself. She

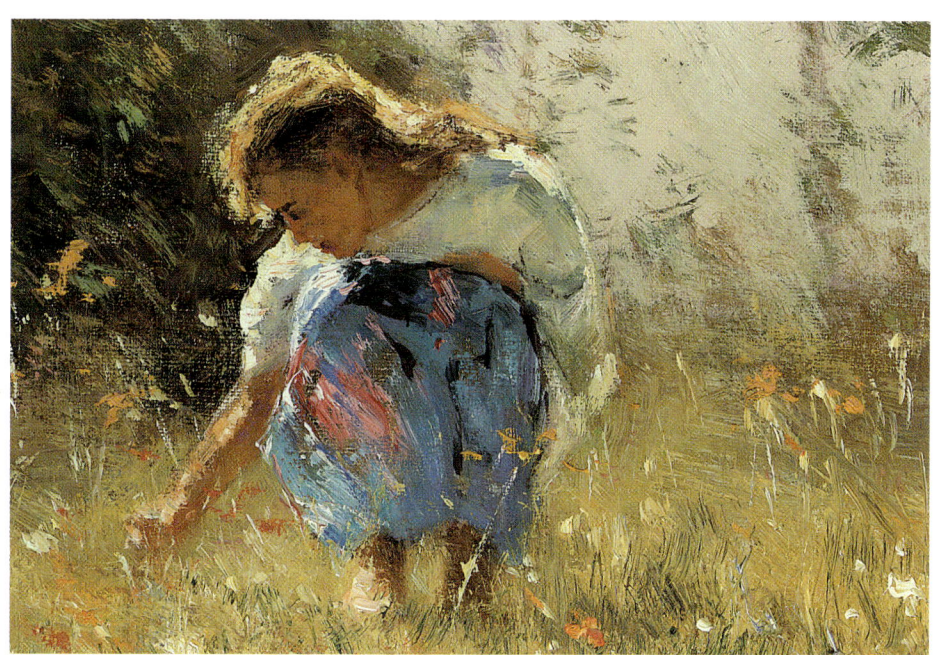

wants to be alone…to let her mind travel ahead in time to life's great adventures, all waiting for her, just around the corner.

"Louise, where have you been?"

And Louise at last takes her place at the table. "Oh, I just went for a walk a little way over there." And she adds with a secret smile, "I didn't go very far."

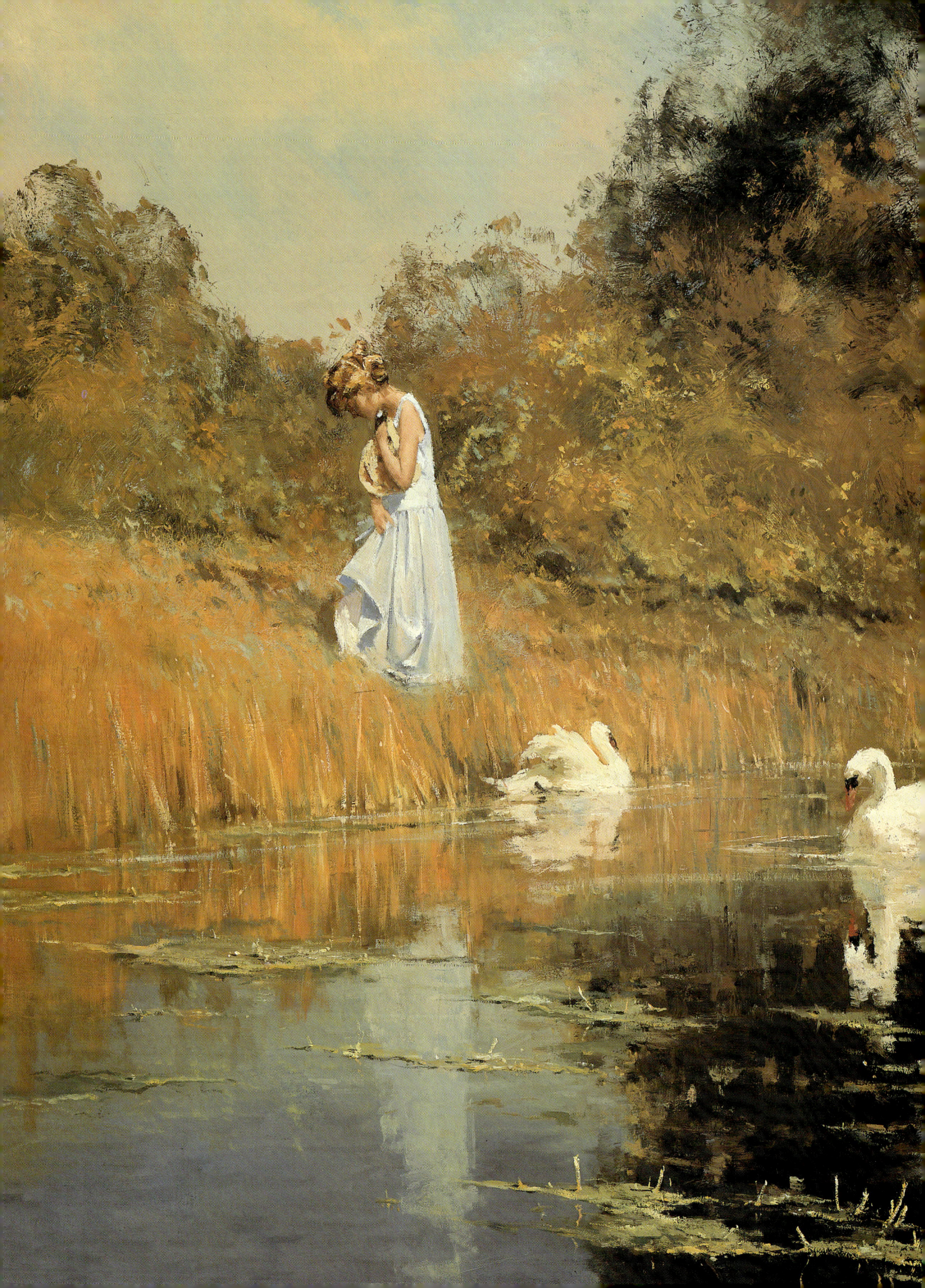

Passing By

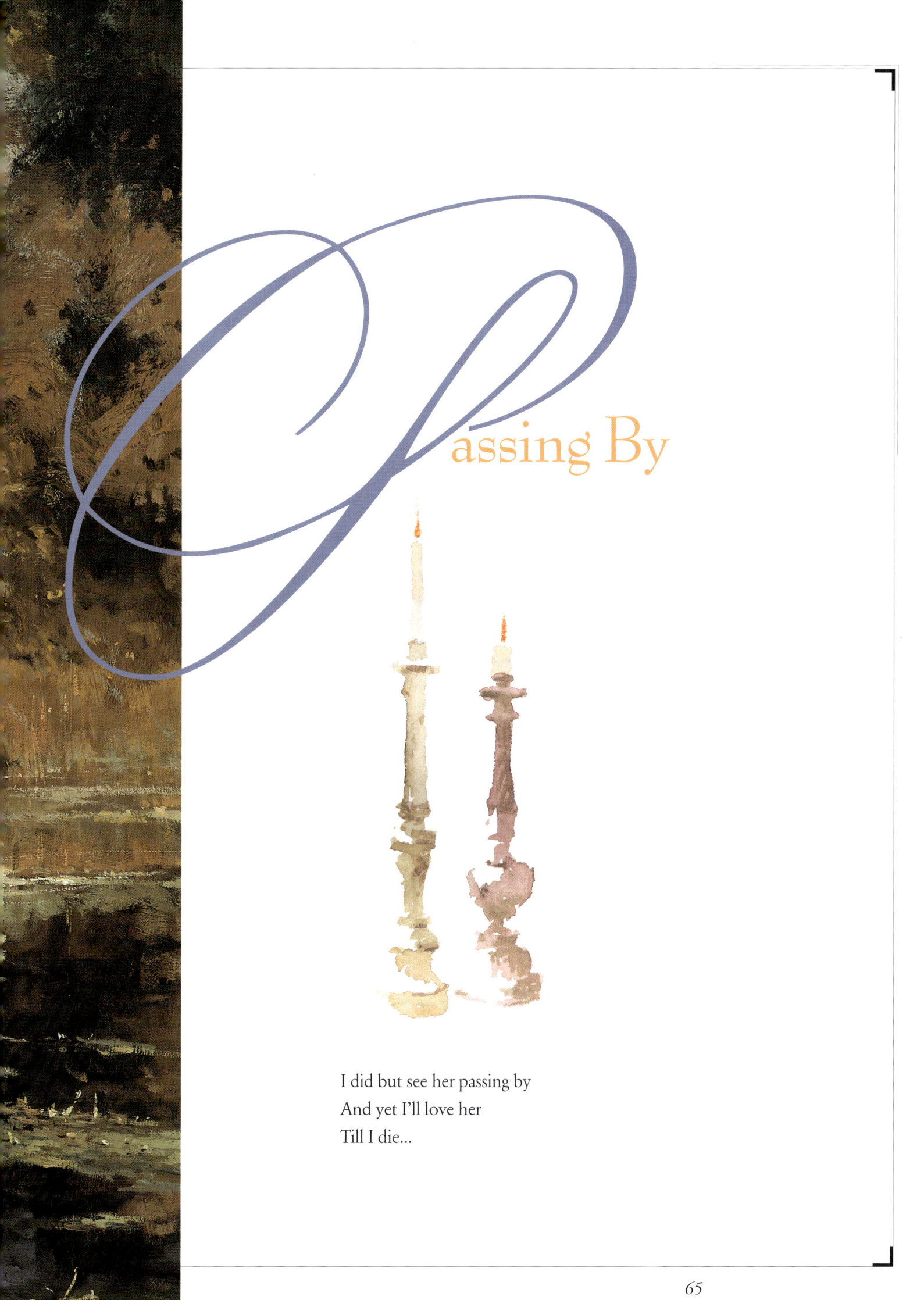

I did but see her passing by
And yet I'll love her
Till I die…

Pink Ribbons

There are few more important bonding moments between a mother and her young daughter than that daily shared experience of combing the child's hair and the tying of the hair ribbons.

It is at private, very intimate times together such as these that an invisible, yet somehow clearly evident "do not disturb" sign confronts any intruder to their space.

It is a time for the child to confide in mother, to seek advice and guidance to help her cope with a whole range of irritating little problems she faces in her own childhood world… "Why is Jenny always picking on me at school?" "Will my teeth always stick out like this?"…"Hate my hair, it's awful."…problems, problems, insurmountable problems. And only Mom can solve them.

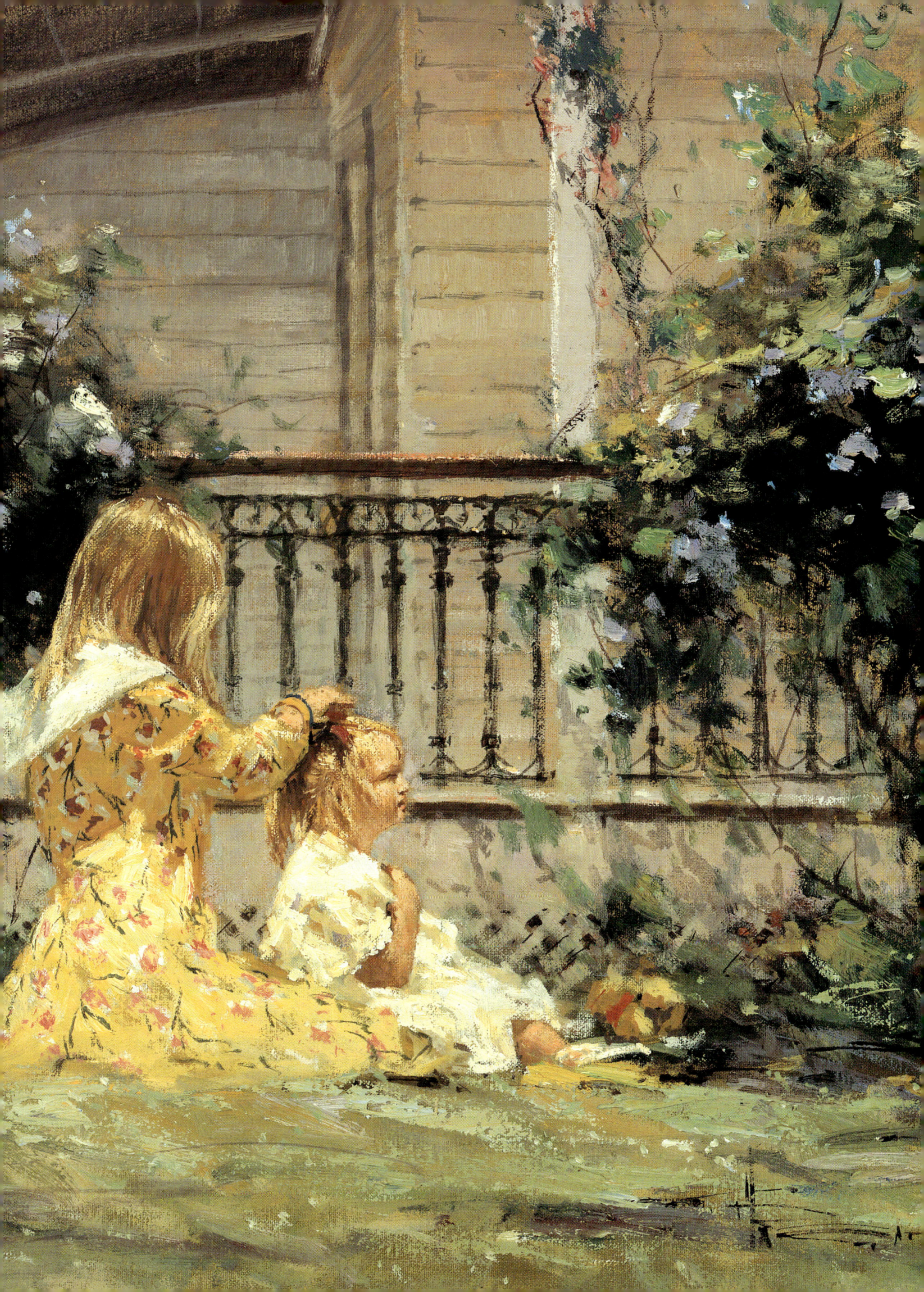

Well, most of them, and especially any problem with the hair.

A little girl of five, just starting school, quickly discovers how important it is to have her hair looking well groomed. She looks around and scrutinizes the hair of other girls her own age. If Julie or Jenny's hair looks better than hers…well, Mommy will simply have to DO something.

So the child sits, while her mother gently wields the comb and brush and then selects just the right ribbons to go with her new party dress. Sitting with her mother in the warmth of the garden, reassured by the comfort of her mother's tender, caring hands.

And the mother. What is on her mind as she wisely consoles and advises the child? Perhaps she recalls a sunny morning, just like this, but years and years ago when she was a child and it was her own flowing locks beings combed and caressed by loving maternal hands. But wait. What were the color of the ribbons on that long ago day? Ah yes, she sees them clearly now. They were pink ribbons, too.

> "And she put me in a party dress
>
> And brushed my long, fair hair
>
> And whispered words of wisdom
>
> In my inattentive ear…"
>
> — KATHERINE WELLESLEY (1858–1897)

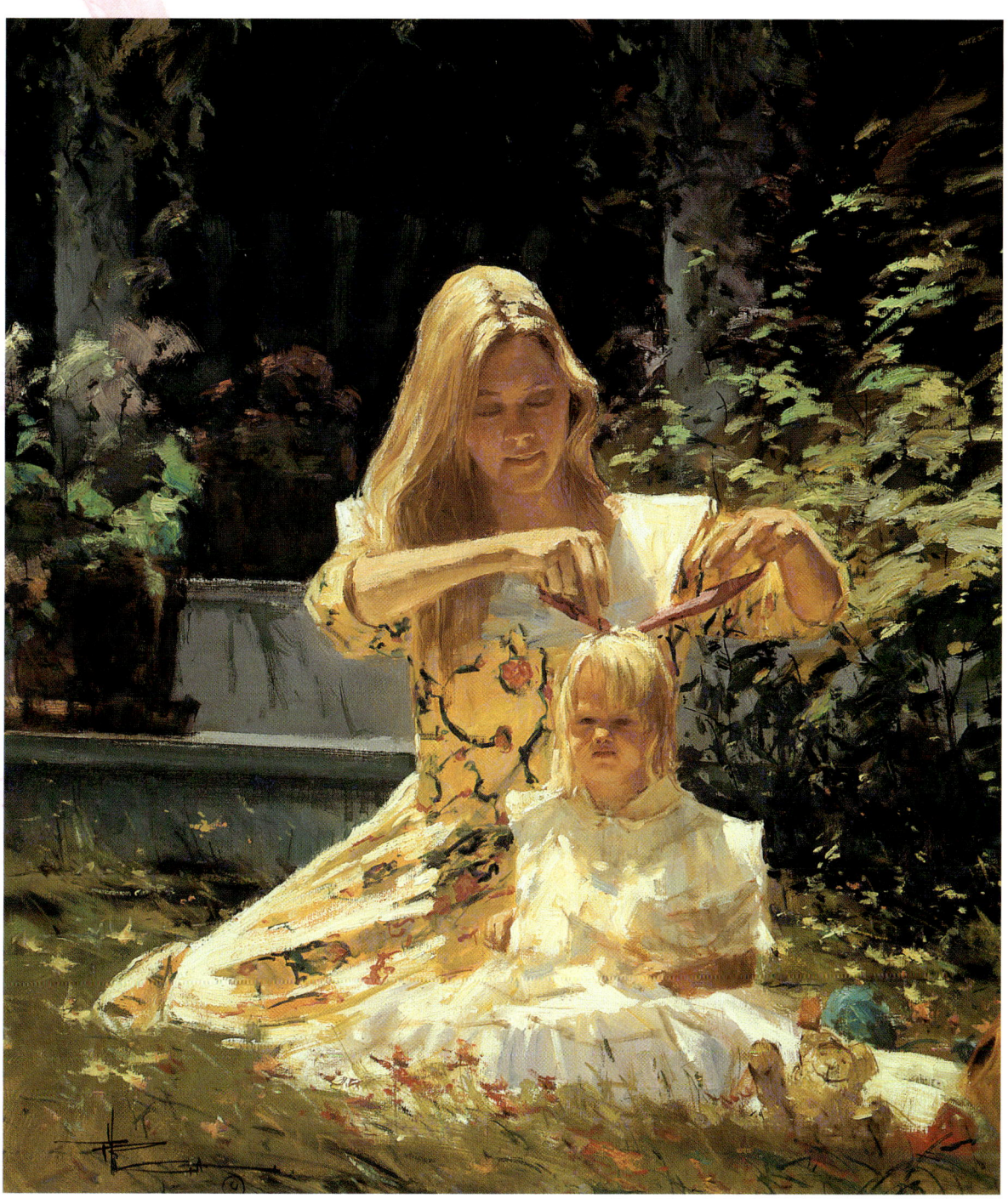

Simple Pleasures

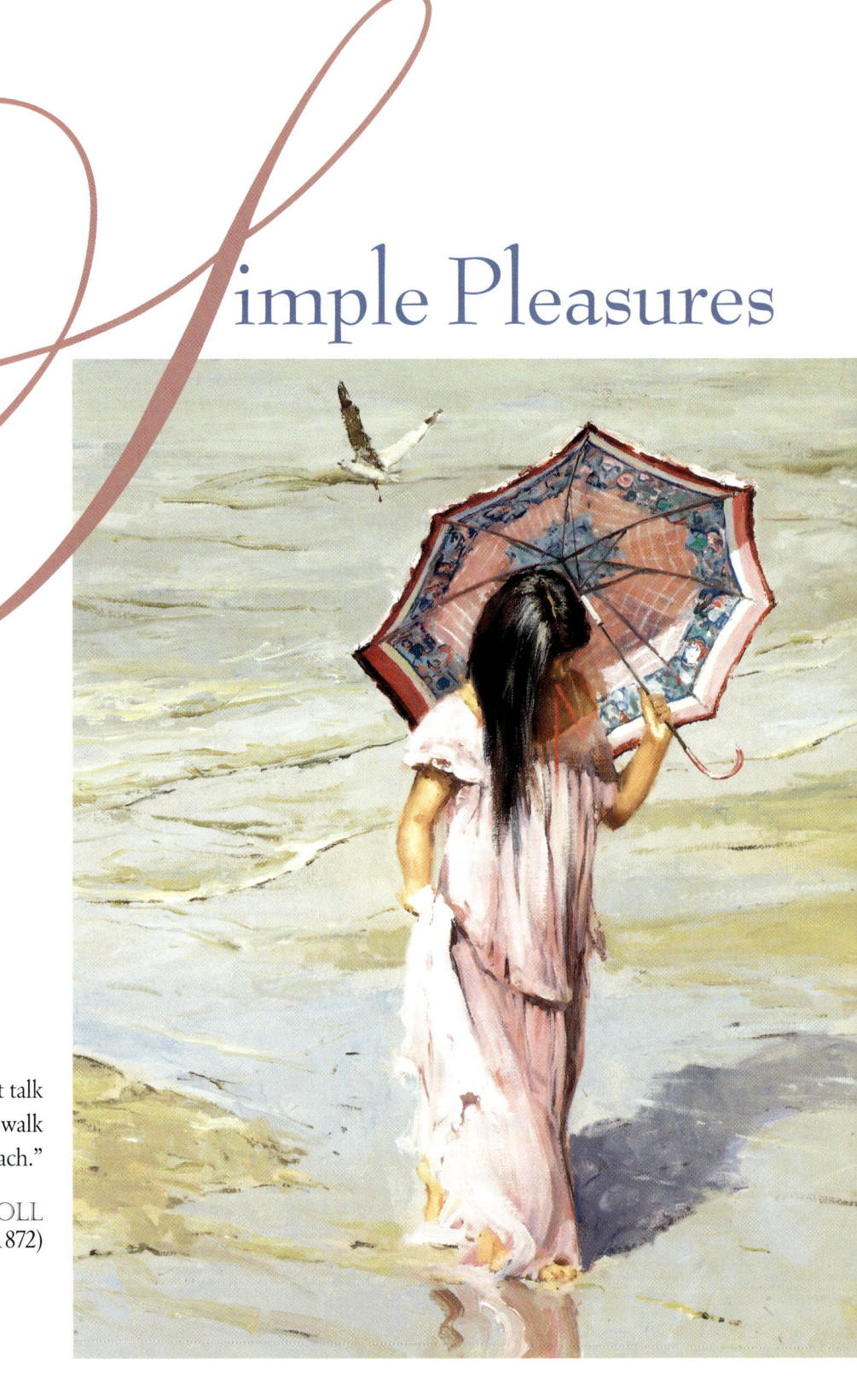

"A pleasant talk
A pleasant walk
Along the briny beach."

—LEWIS CARROLL
(THE WALRUS AND THE CARPENTER, 1872)

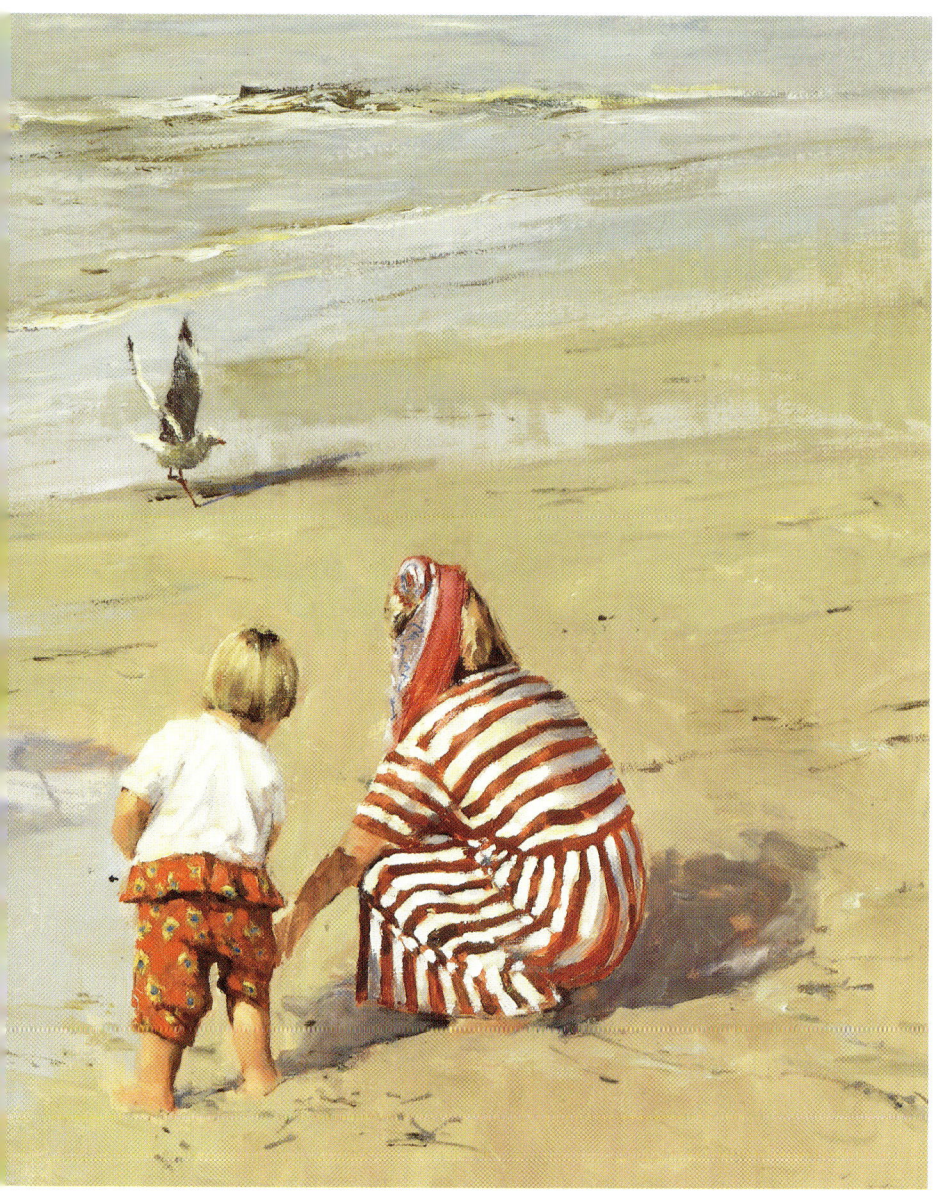

"Little drops of water
Little grains of sand
Make the mighty ocean
And the pleasant land."

—JULIA FLETCHER CARNEY
 (1845)

First Born

"There's somethin' about the first born," confessed the mother of five in a soft, almost whispering voice. "Every night, when I turn off the light, it's that first one that I'm always thinkin' about and worryin' about…in those last seconds just before I close my eyes and go to sleep."

Then she added, with a resigned shrug and a rueful smile, "And I know that's what I'll be doin' even on the day I die."

By chance I happened to overhear that very revealing and intimate admission between two obviously motherly women. Both were in their mid-50s and had lovely life-lined faces. We were all travelling in a New York subway several years ago. It was just a little snippet of verbal trivia that goes in one ear and out the other. But this time, for once, it stayed locked securely inside my head.

As an artist, the words I overheard intrigued me greatly. I started thinking there and then that in the future, whenever I came across a mother with her first born child, I should observe the mother's expression a little more closely. Perhaps there was something in that expression I might not have quite captured in my several previous mother-with-child paintings.

> *Once in royal David's city*
> *Stood a lowly cattle shed*
> *Where a Mother laid her baby*
> *In a manger for his bed.*
>
> — CECIL FRANCES ALEXANDER (1818–1895)

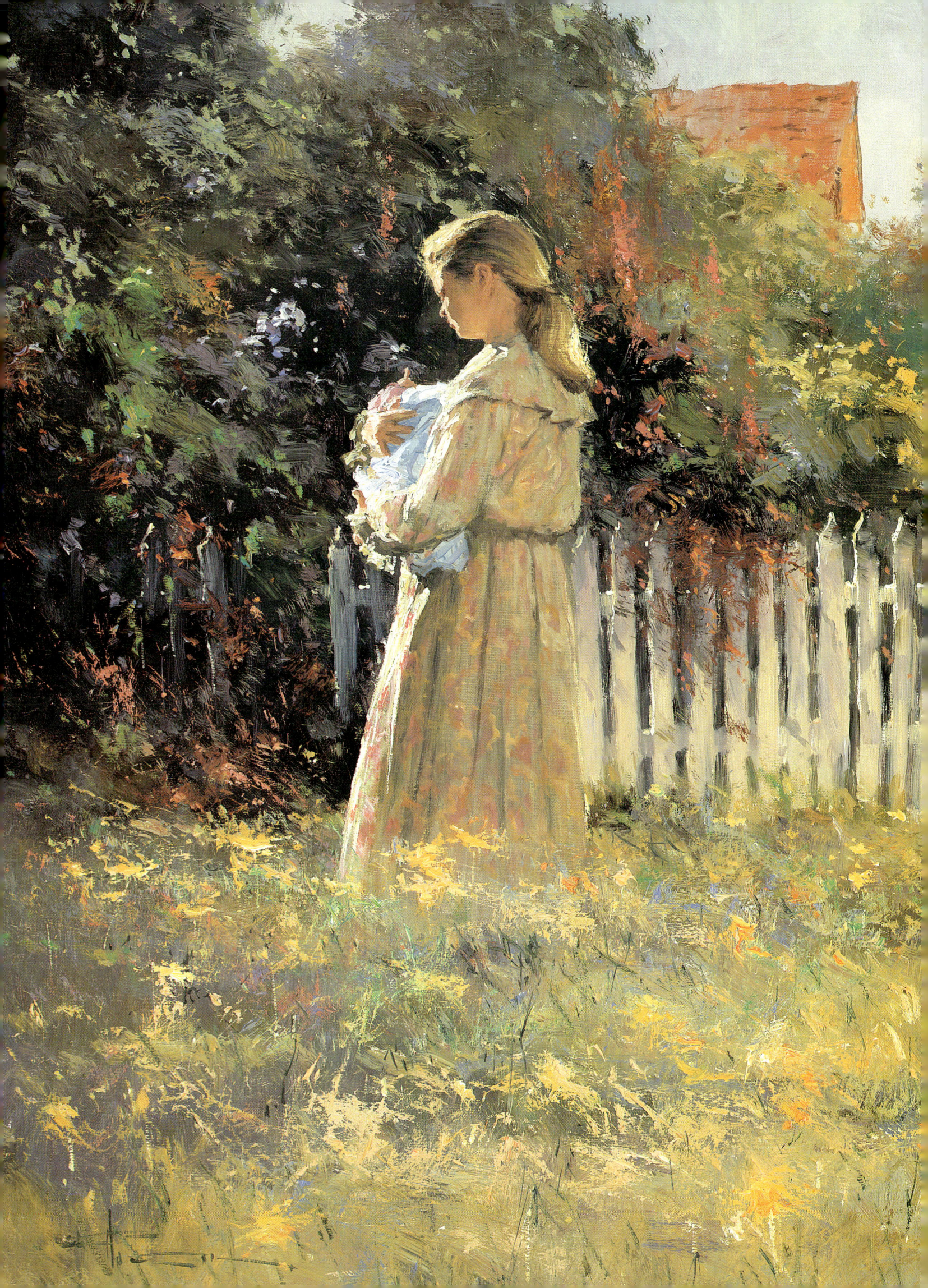

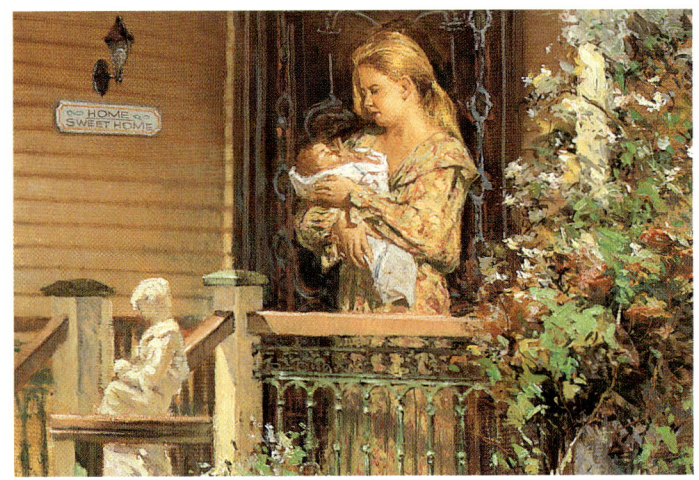

As it happens, I have three children of my own, but still, as a mere male, I freely concede there is a mystical psychic bond between a mother and her brood – and especially between a mother and her first born. This is a mystery that no mere male in the world can ever really comprehend. Certainly, until I chanced to overhear that New York subway conversation all those years ago, I confess I had not entirely appreciated the primordial importance of every mother's feelings concerning her very first born. Now, my eyes are much more open on this profound subject.

I was able to take advantage of this new awareness of mine on a recent painting expedition to Georgia where I was fortunate enough to meet a very friendly and likeable young married couple.

I was passing through a little town in the northwest of the state when I stopped to get some gas for my battered old Jeep Landrover. A young guy was running the small filling station that I pulled into. He noticed my painting equipment in the back seat and it turned out he was a hobby artist himself, so we got to talking. He invited me to drop over to his house and have a look at his painting efforts.

As he opened the front gate, I looked up at the house and a warm feeling came over me immediately because it was one of those very comfortable, old style, all-timber, unpretentious country homes that greets you with a sincere and opened-armed welcome.

"Honey!" the young man called to his wife, "Come on out here – we got company." A few seconds later she came out onto the front porch, with her first born baby in her arms. She didn't look at me for a few moments, she was still gazing intently at her baby with that indescribable gaze that I now realized I had only ever seen before in exactly these same situatuons.

It was an eternal scene as old as the human race itself: A mother gazing down in complete adoration…at her first born child.

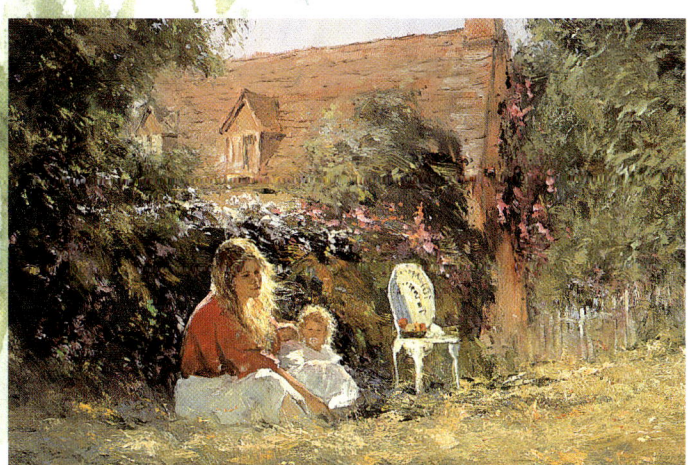

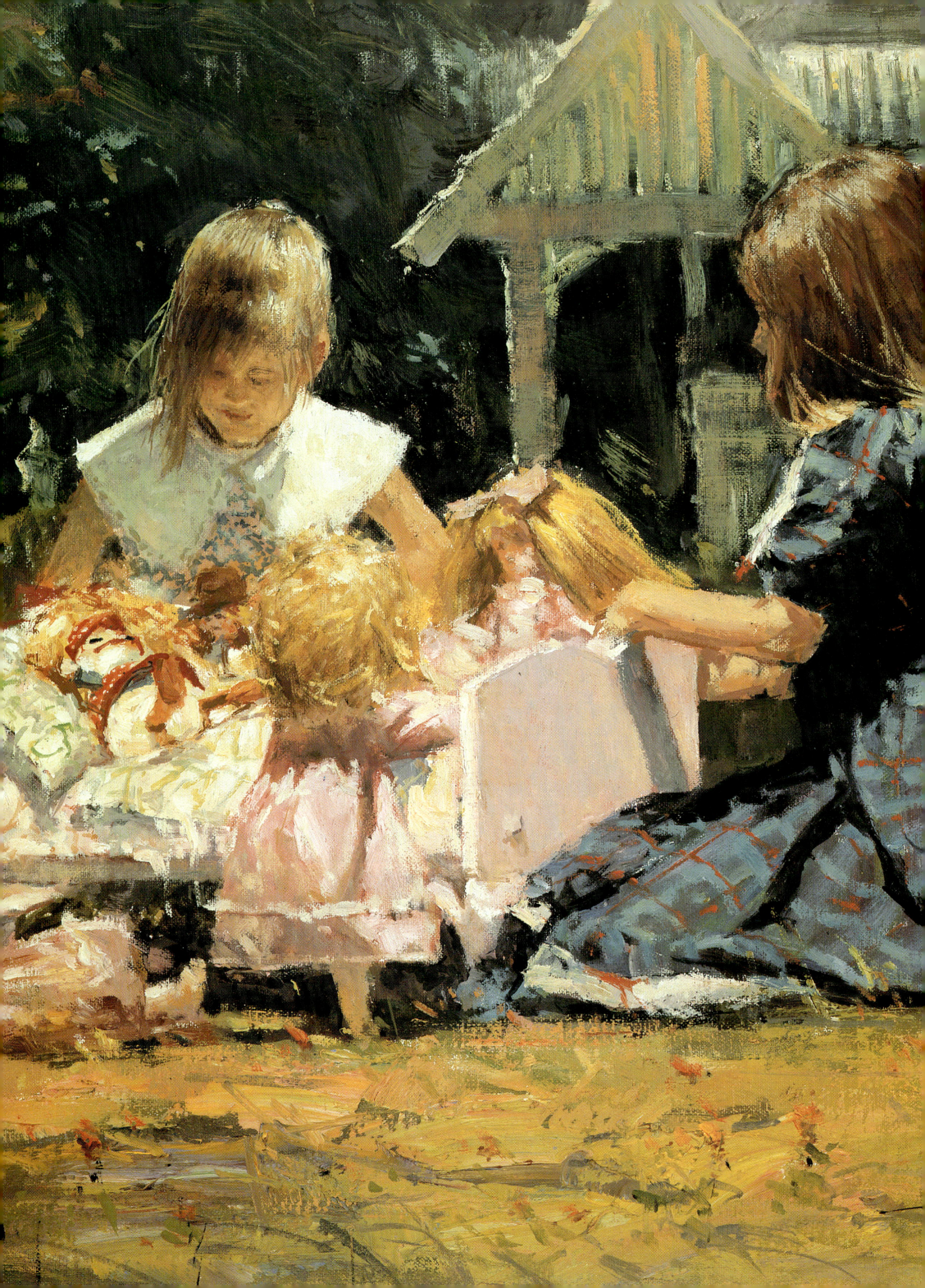

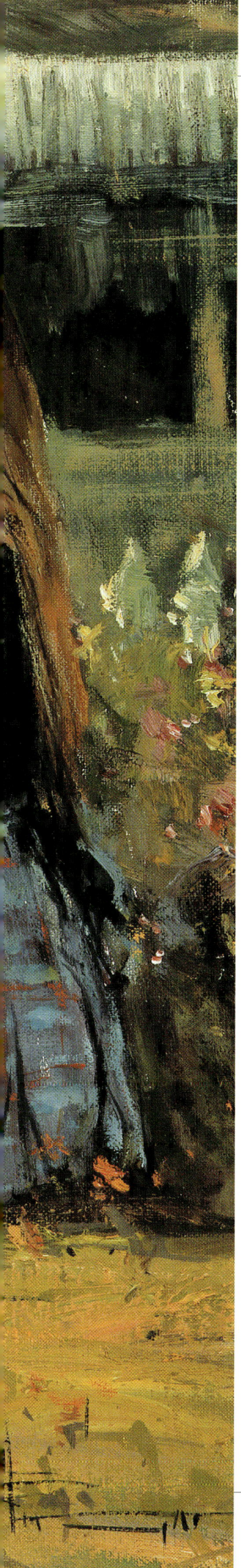

Little Mothers

They have names for all their dolls named after their playmates at school – Julie, Linda, Rebecca, whatever. Sometimes the dolls are naughty and receive gentle smacks on their little plastic bottoms. "You young ladies had just better behave yourselves," comes the stern reprimand from one of the doll's little mothers. "Otherwise you'll get no more pocket money for a week!"

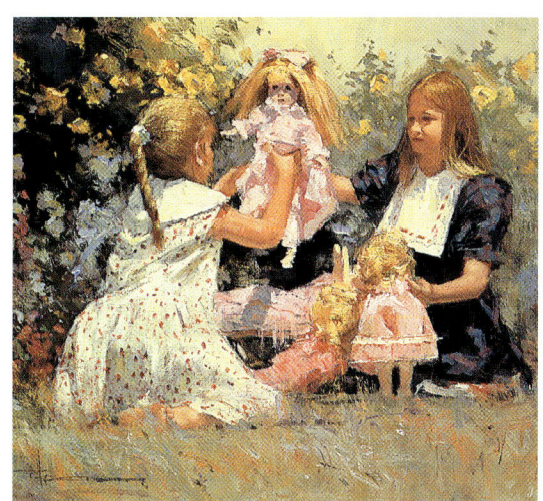

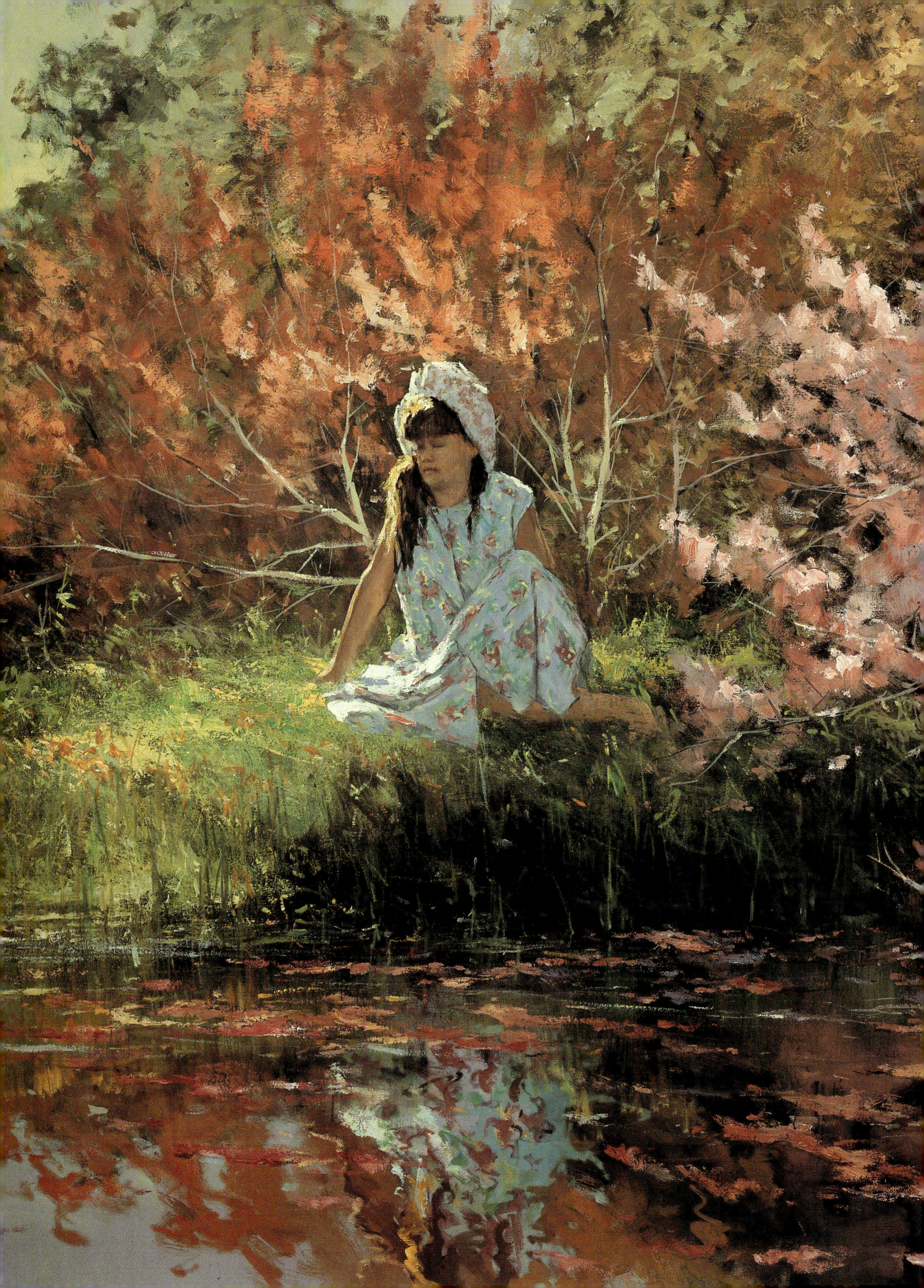

WAITING

Many years ago I happened to read somewhere that the teenage years for a girl could aptly be described as the waiting years.

Waiting? At first I did not fully understand this description – they're uncertain years, of course, even difficult years, but 'waiting' years? Waiting for what in particular? It is only now that I have a teenage daughter of my own, that I come to realize that the word 'waiting' has a very special meaning for girls of tender years champing at the bit of life's adventures.

Waiting. Now I've finally become keenly aware that perhaps no other word is so appropriate for them. They are always waiting for something to happen, and the waiting usually begins, not surprisingly, when they first discover boys.

Waiting. At their junior prom they wait, with handkerchiefs dabbing their perspiring palms, for their first invitation to dance. Admittedly, the personality girls and the really pretty ones don't have to wait too long at all. But some girls have to just sit and wait. And wait and wait and wait.

Waiting. Those hours in front of the mirror, anxiously studying the spots on their cheeks and waiting so impatiently for them to disappear. And, of course, there is the anxious waiting for the pubescent changes in their figure – changes they fear will never come. Waiting. They wait for the telephone to ring to be asked out on their first date. Then the longed-for date finally takes place and sometimes, of course, it is a terrible disappointment – which often means they are still left waiting for their first good night kiss.

A little later and again they are waiting. Waiting for the right boy to come along...to go steady, if that's not too old-fashioned an expression these days.

Waiting. And even when the teenage years are gone, it seems the waiting and yearning still persist. Waiting for the engagement ring to be slipped on her finger and then...the longest, waiting of all. The waiting for the wearing of the magical white dress on that one fairytale day she has always dreamed about...and waited for.

In the meantime. Until all this comes to pass, she sits and stares at her reflection and waits. So impatient for something to happen.

"You are young and have the world before you.
Stoop as you go through it
And you will miss many hard bumps."

—Those famous parental words of advice have been offered to generations of American teenage boys and girls. I was surprised to learn that they were originally given in the early 18th century to a then very young Benjamin Franklin as he was approaching a low-hanging beam in a parsonage.

Coming Home

"I'll be home for Christmas"… so go the very meaningful opening lyrics from a wonderful old song by Bing Crosby.

But if we happen to be based far from our roots, it's not only at Christmastime that our thoughts turn longingly to that one place that is the source of all our inner securities. Home is the link to our growing-up past, our rock solid foundation base, our permanent shelter from life's stormy seasons.

Recently I had a conversation with someone with long experience in the popular music industry. It surprised me not at all to discover that the word "home" is one of the three most commonly used nouns in modern song lyrics. Can you guess the other two words? If not, I'll pass them on. The other words are "love" and "heart."

> "So it's home again, and home again
> America for me
> My heart is turning home again
> And there I long to be."
>
> — HENRY VAN DYKE
> (1852–1933)

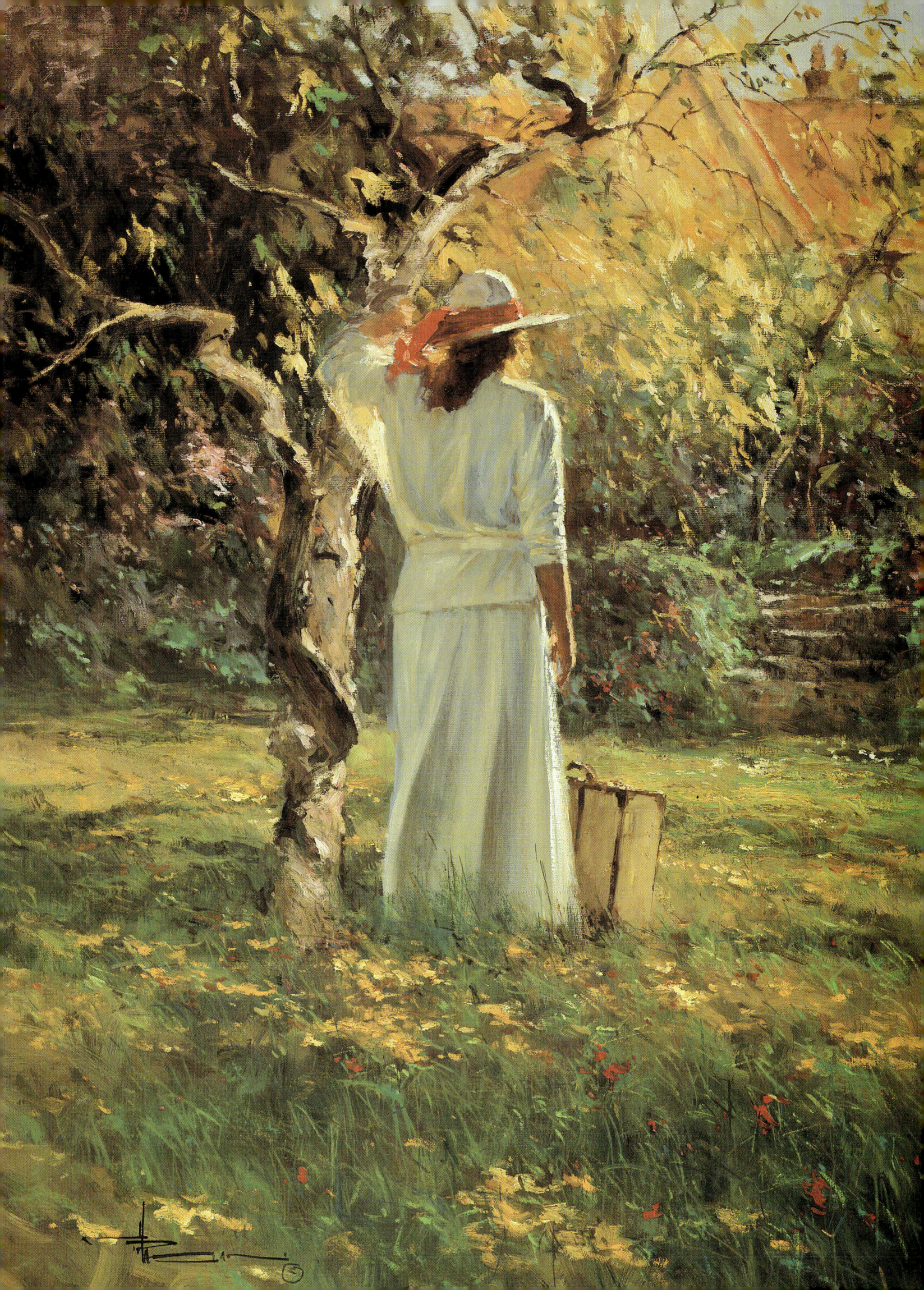

"Where we love is home
Home that our feet may leave
But not our hearts."

— Oliver Wendell Holmes
(1809–1894)

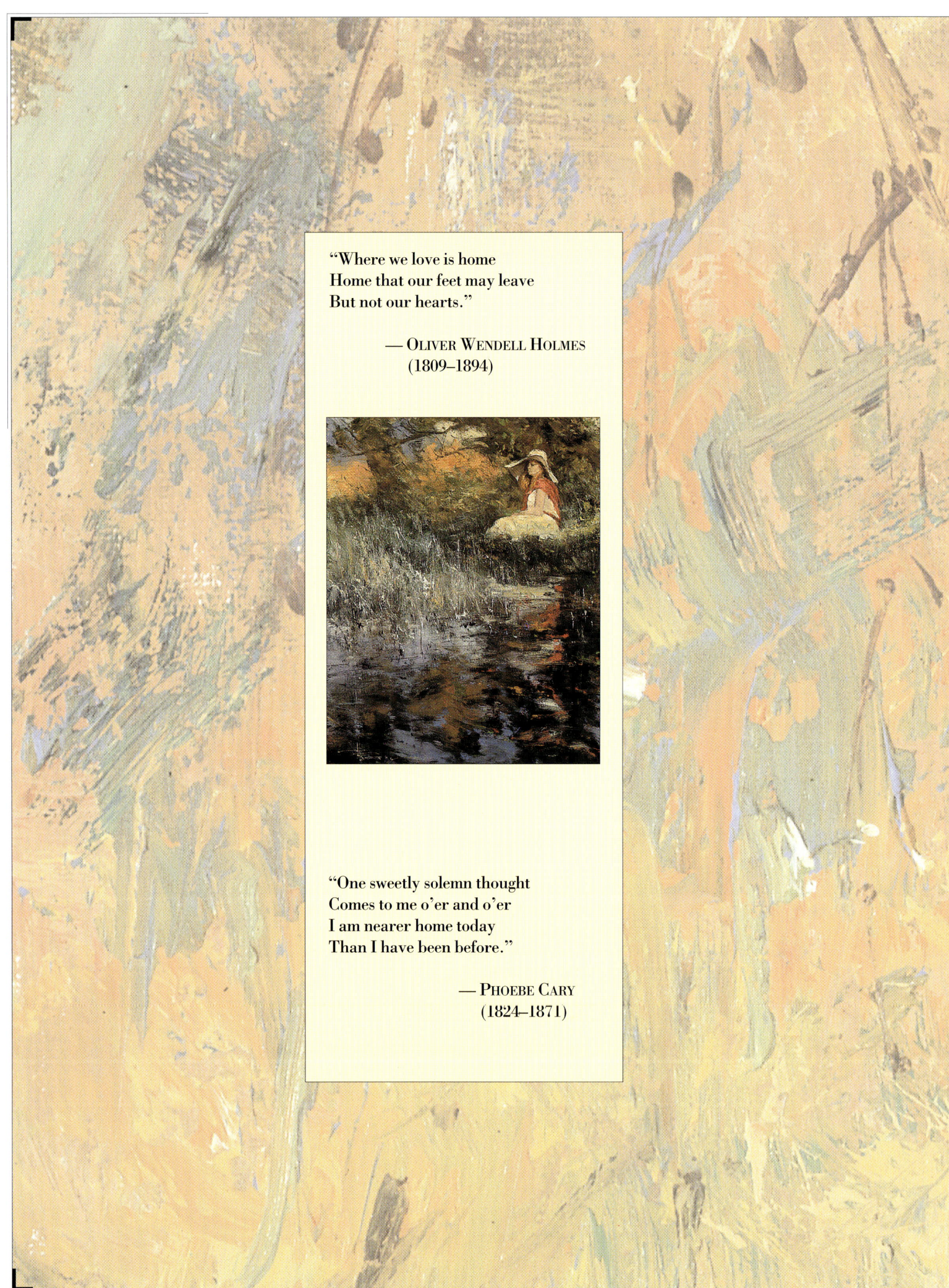

"One sweetly solemn thought
Comes to me o'er and o'er
I am nearer home today
Than I have been before."

— Phoebe Cary
(1824–1871)

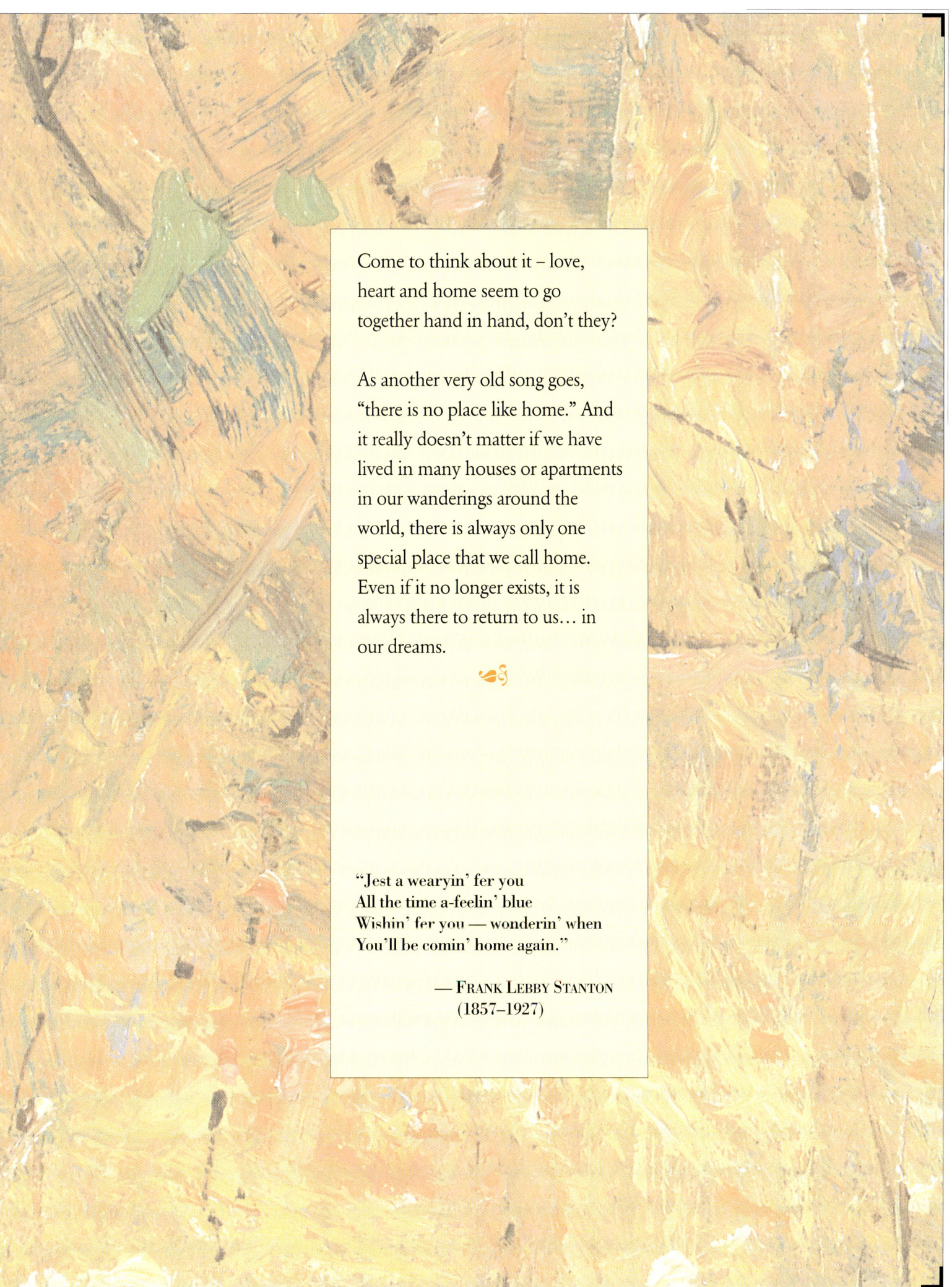

Come to think about it – love, heart and home seem to go together hand in hand, don't they?

As another very old song goes, "there is no place like home." And it really doesn't matter if we have lived in many houses or apartments in our wanderings around the world, there is always only one special place that we call home. Even if it no longer exists, it is always there to return to us… in our dreams.

"Jest a wearyin' fer you
All the time a-feelin' blue
Wishin' fer you — wonderin' when
You'll be comin' home again."

— FRANK LEBBY STANTON
(1857–1927)

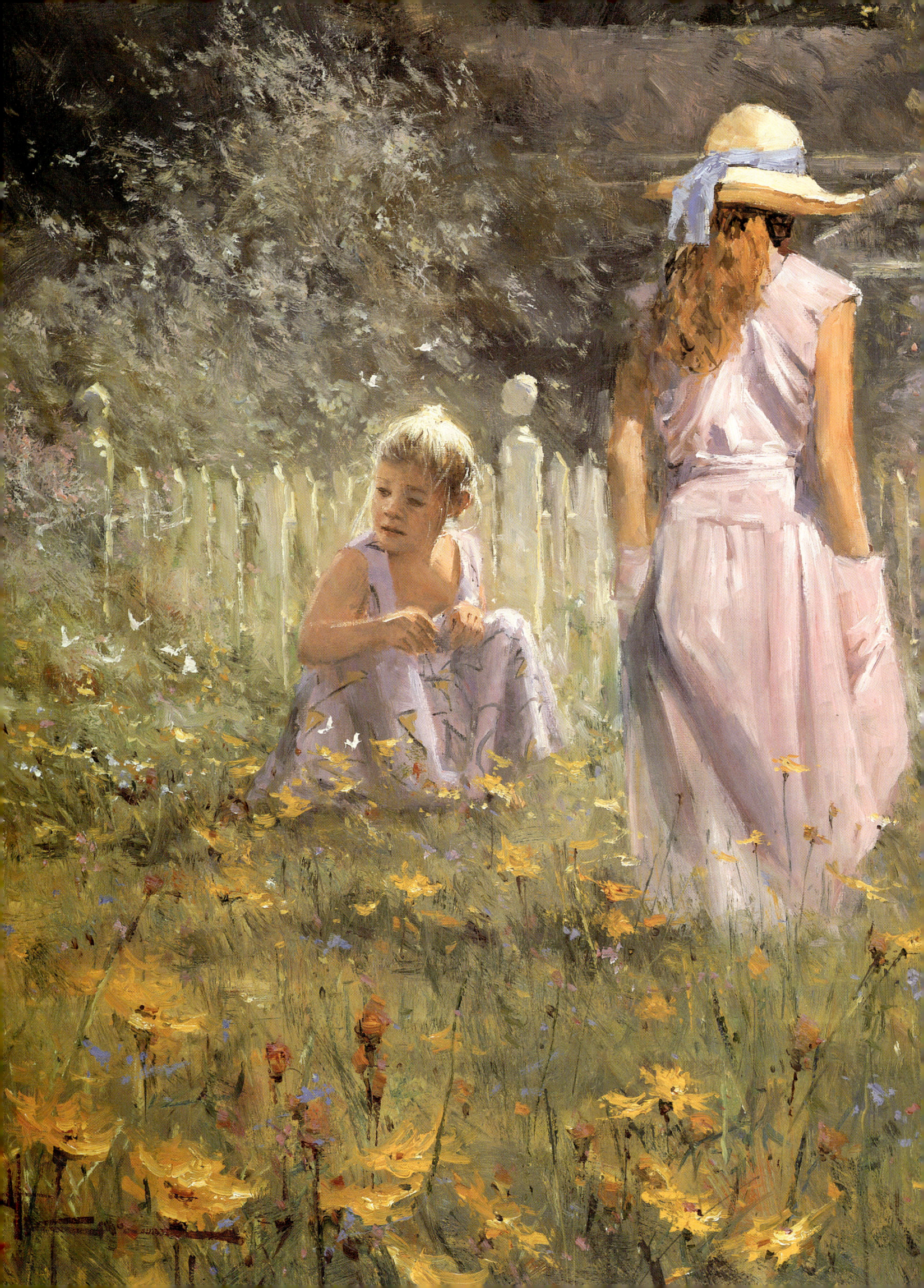

The Child And The Butterfly

The inquisitive small child asks:
"What is a butterfly?"
For the answer we reach for the textbook
On the shelf
A butterfly is an insect, we answer matter-of-factly
An insect which flies by day and rests at night
With its wings held together.

The child asks again:
"Why do I get this powdery stuff
On my hands when I catch a butterfly?"

We refer to the textbook again:
That happens because the two pairs of
Wings on a butterfly have a powdery covering
Of scales, which are there for
The purpose of reflecting light.

The child isn't finished with us yet.
"Why do some butterflies have funny looking
Stripes and circles on their wings?"
We dig deeper into the textbook:
It says that the striking patterns
On butterflies are used in recognition
Of each other and often as
A camouflage protection.

How long do butterflies live? the child asks
This time we don't need the textbook.
Unfortunately, butterflies don't hang around
This mortal coil too long, kiddo.
Sorry, but after a few days
It's Bye Bye Butterfly.

The child is sad. But still manages
One more question.
"Do butterflies go to heaven?"
Again, we don't need the textbook.
Yup. As a matter of fact, that's their home town.
There's billions and trillions of 'em up there!

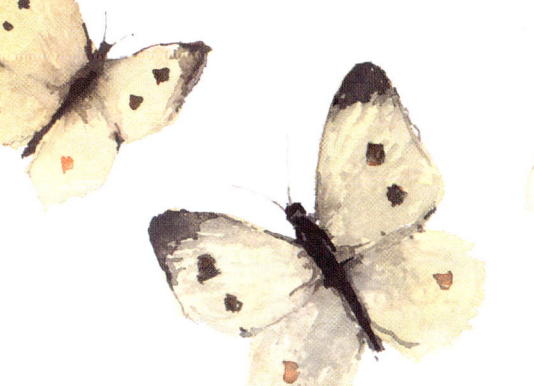

The child smiles.

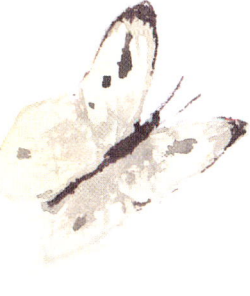

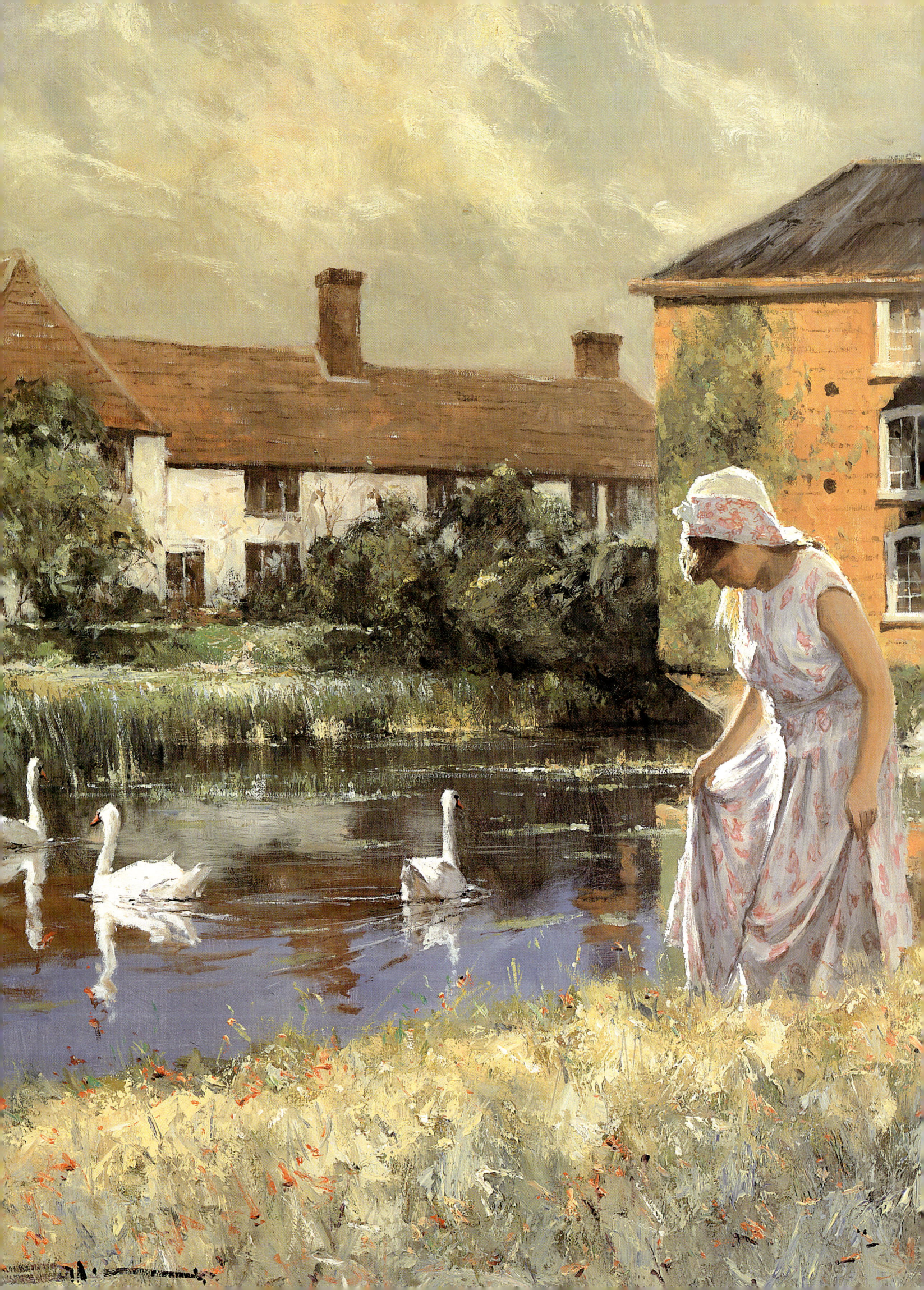

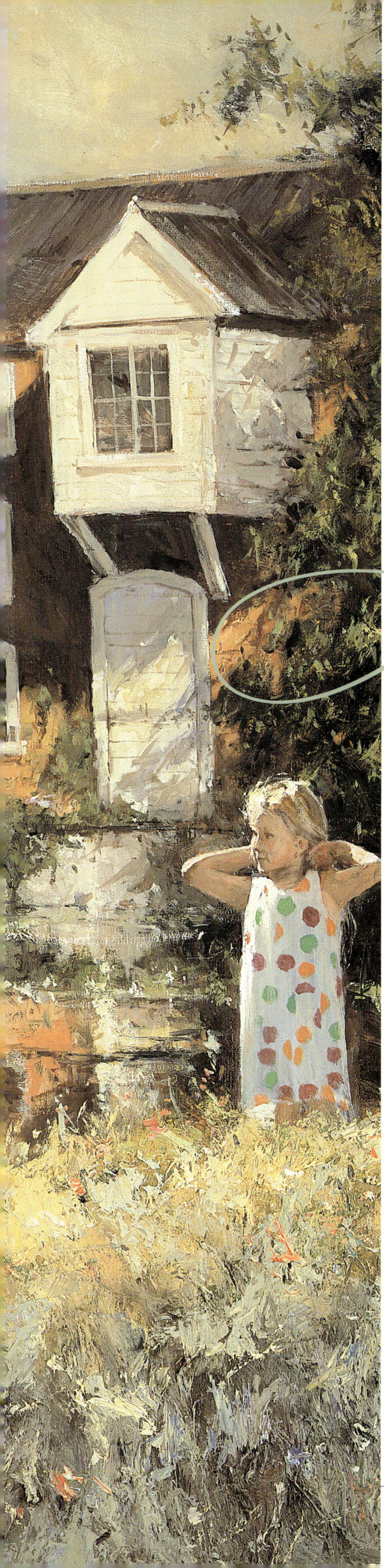

Joy

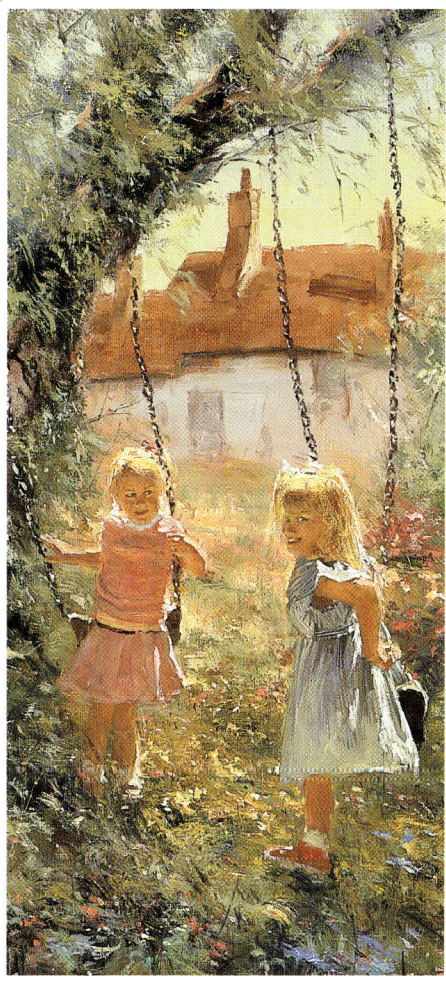

I am gone into the fields
To take what this sweet hour yields

— SHELLEY
(1792–1892)

BIRTHDAY PARTY

"Daddy, will you get me a clown for my birthday? There was a terrific clown at Melanie's birthday last month, so can I…may I…have one too…please, Daddy, please?"

When a seven-year-old girl says please, in a certain wide-eyed imploring way, and with a little smile that shows the tooth on the right side that's starting to wobble a bit…that's when she gets her poor old Dad right over the plate. Okay, if it's a clown she wants, she's got it. No problem.

When my pal Larry was faced with this request from his adored little princess, he certainly didn't think it would present much of a problem.

"Green grow the rashes, O
Green grows the rashes, O
The sweetest hours that are I spend
Are spent among the lessees. O."

— ROBERT BURNS
(1759–1796)

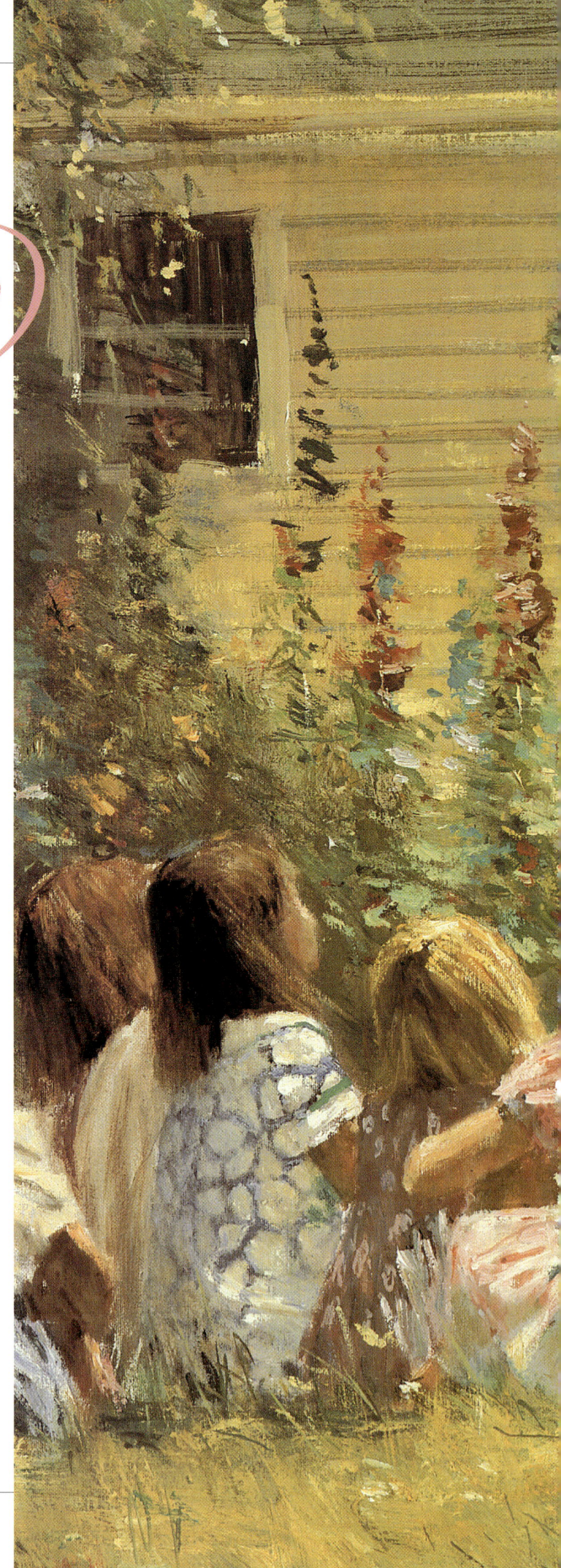

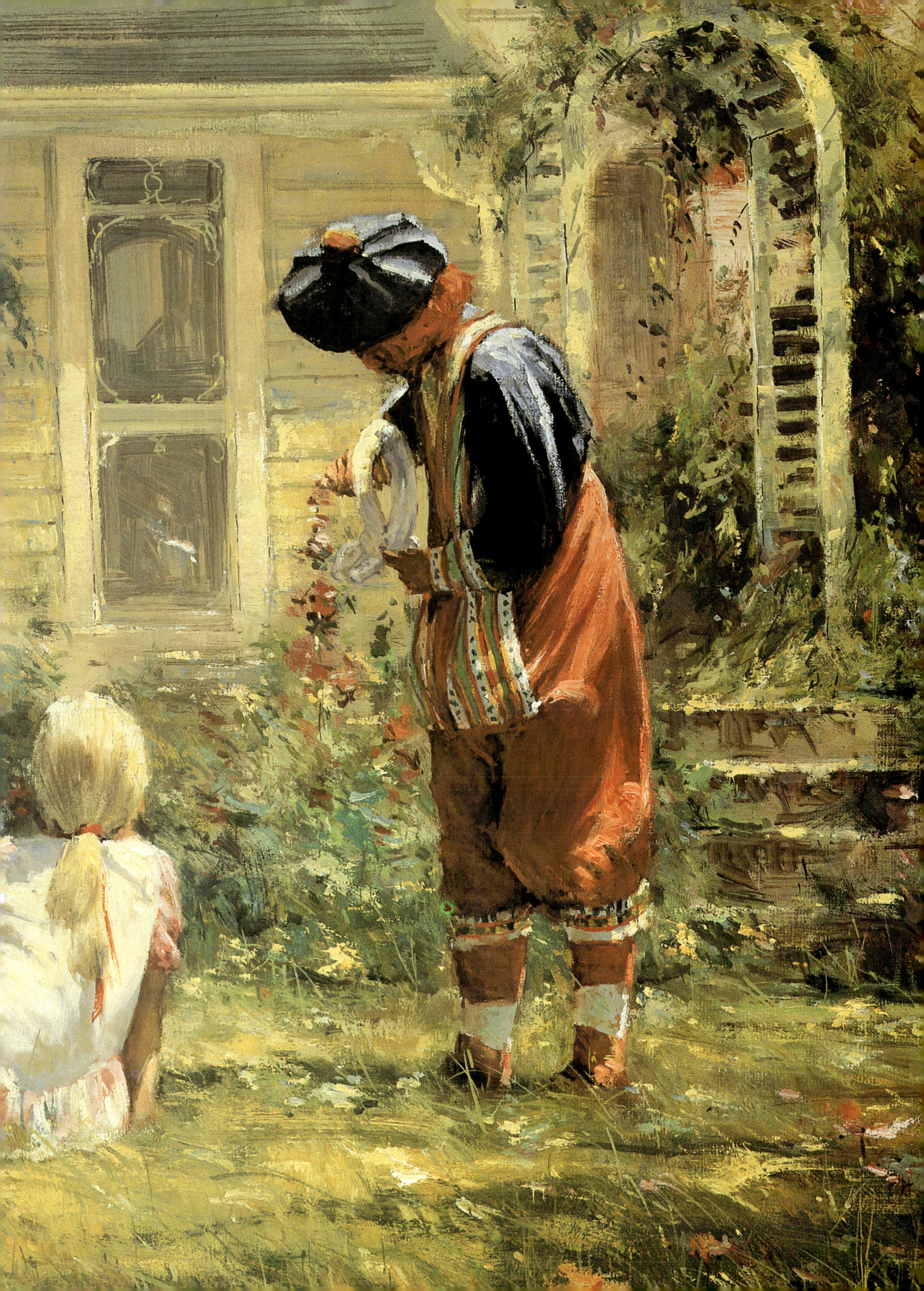

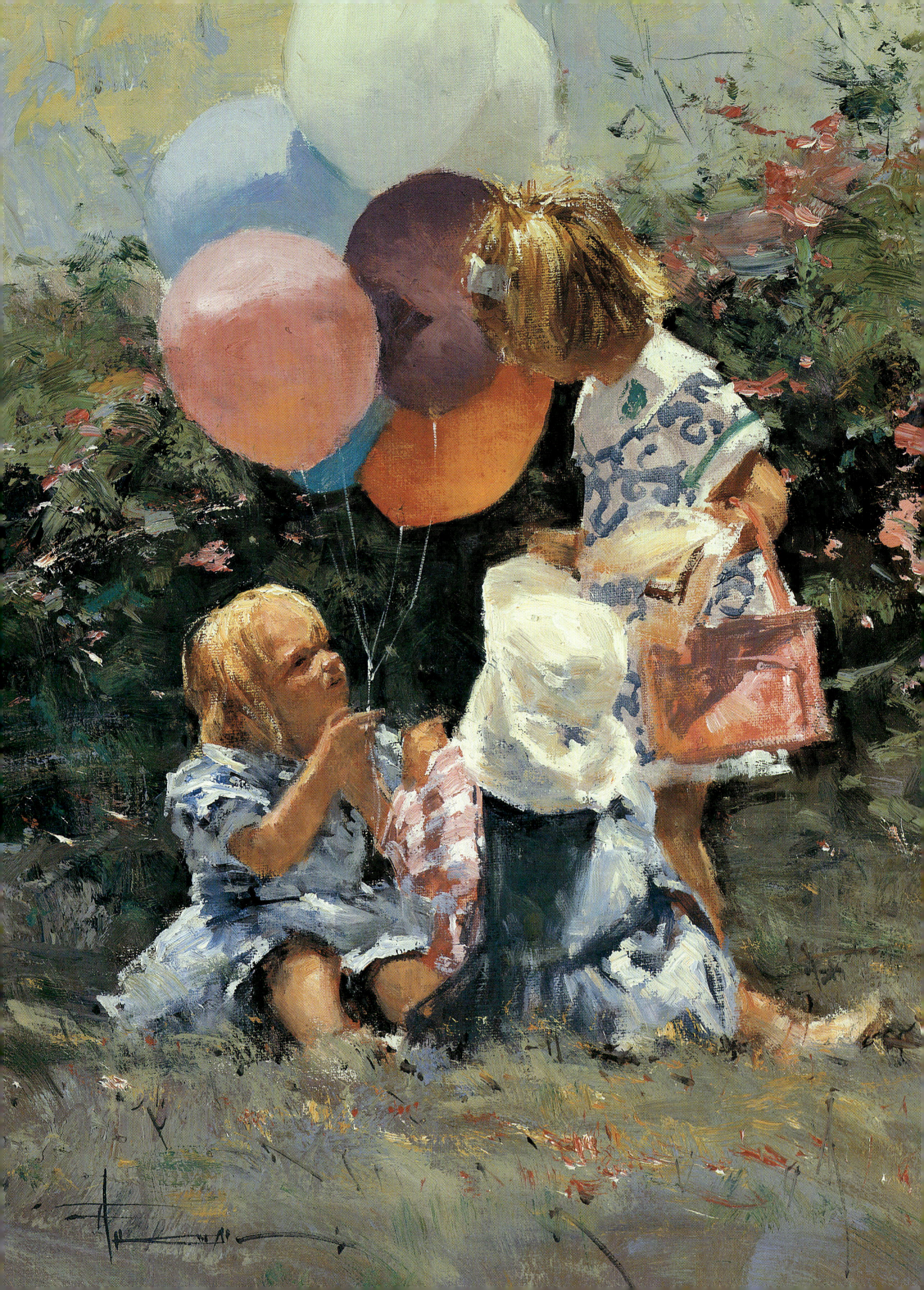

But little did he know of the dramas awaiting him. The way he describes it must have turned out to be one of the major crises of his life.

The trouble started as soon as Larry got on the telephone to an agency that handles these kind of bookings and was informed that his daughter's birthday happened to fall on the day of the annual magicians' convention. And, as most clowns are usually also magicians, there wasn't an available professional clown in town. Send in the clowns? Not as easy as it sounds.

Comes the morning of the birthday party, and Larry is still completely clownless and rapidly approaching total panic. It was to be a small party because he'd only just moved into the neighborhood, and his little girl hadn't had enough time to find many new playmates. But her best friend, Melanie, was definitely coming and she had promised Melanie that there would be a clown without fail, even adding a solemn cross of the heart and hope to die.

Somehow poor Larry tried to find a clown – or else face the dire consequences of a seven-year-old daughter's terrifying wrath.

That's when Larry had a brain wave. He suddenly remembered the old Scottish janitor at his office was a former vaudeville comedian back home in Scotland. His name was Angus McSomething, but Larry only knew him as Jock, the way we seem to call all Scottish people in America. When Larry telephoned him, he whispered a silent prayer while he waited for Jock's answer. The prayer must have helped, because Jock said, sure, he'd love to do it.

Furthermore, he promised to put on the best clown's act these kids would ever see.

Well, they say you can always rely on a Scotty and Jock was as good as his word. He turned up in the wackiest clown's outfit you ever saw – a crazy, wonderful Scottish clown he was. Even though his accent was so thick the kids hardly understood a word, they didn't mind at all. Jock was a laugh a minute. He carried a bag over his shoulder and kept pulling out all kinds of magical tricks, white rabbits, walking sticks, colored ribbon twenty feet long. He even produced a rubber crocodile that said, "Who wants to be my breakfast?"

He enchanted the kids and they squealed with ecstatic delight at every marvelous surprise he produced.

They simply adored him.

Jock put forty years of slapstick showbiz and everything else he knew into his act and was exhausted at the end of it, but he said he had the time of his life. So Larry took him inside and gratefully poured him a drop of Jock's favorite national beverage. "Here's to America's greatest ally," said Larry. "Scotland."

With a profound sense of relief, that only a father who has somehow delivered the goods on his kid's birthday could possibly understand, Larry happily clinked glasses with the funny old clown in the tartan kilt.

Recollections

How dear to this heart are
the scenes of my
childhood
When fond
recollection presents
them to view

— SAMUEL
WOODWORTH
(1785–1892)

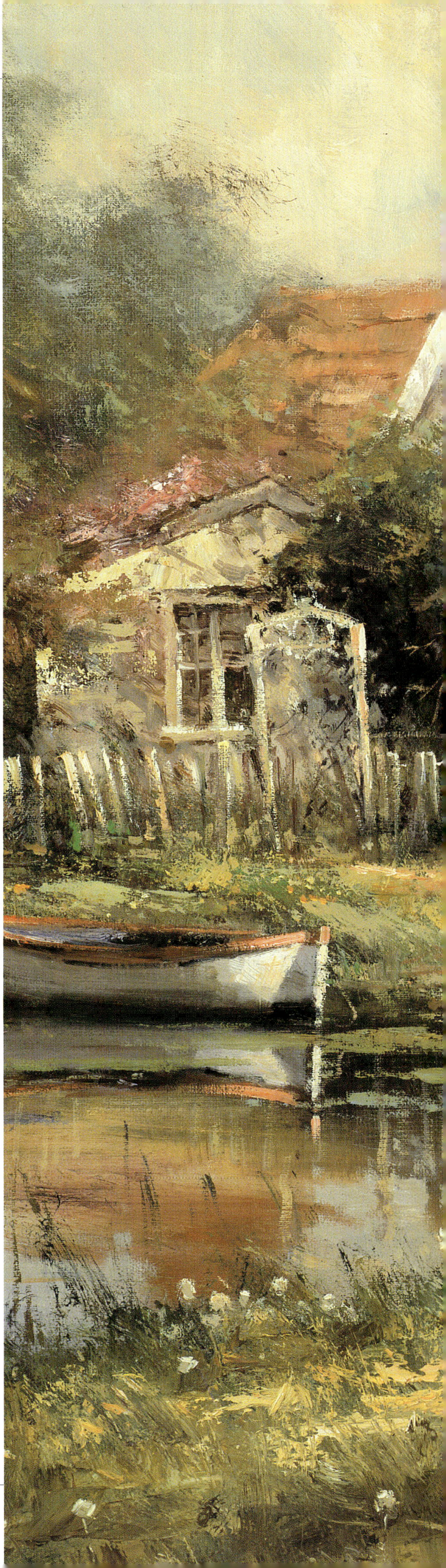

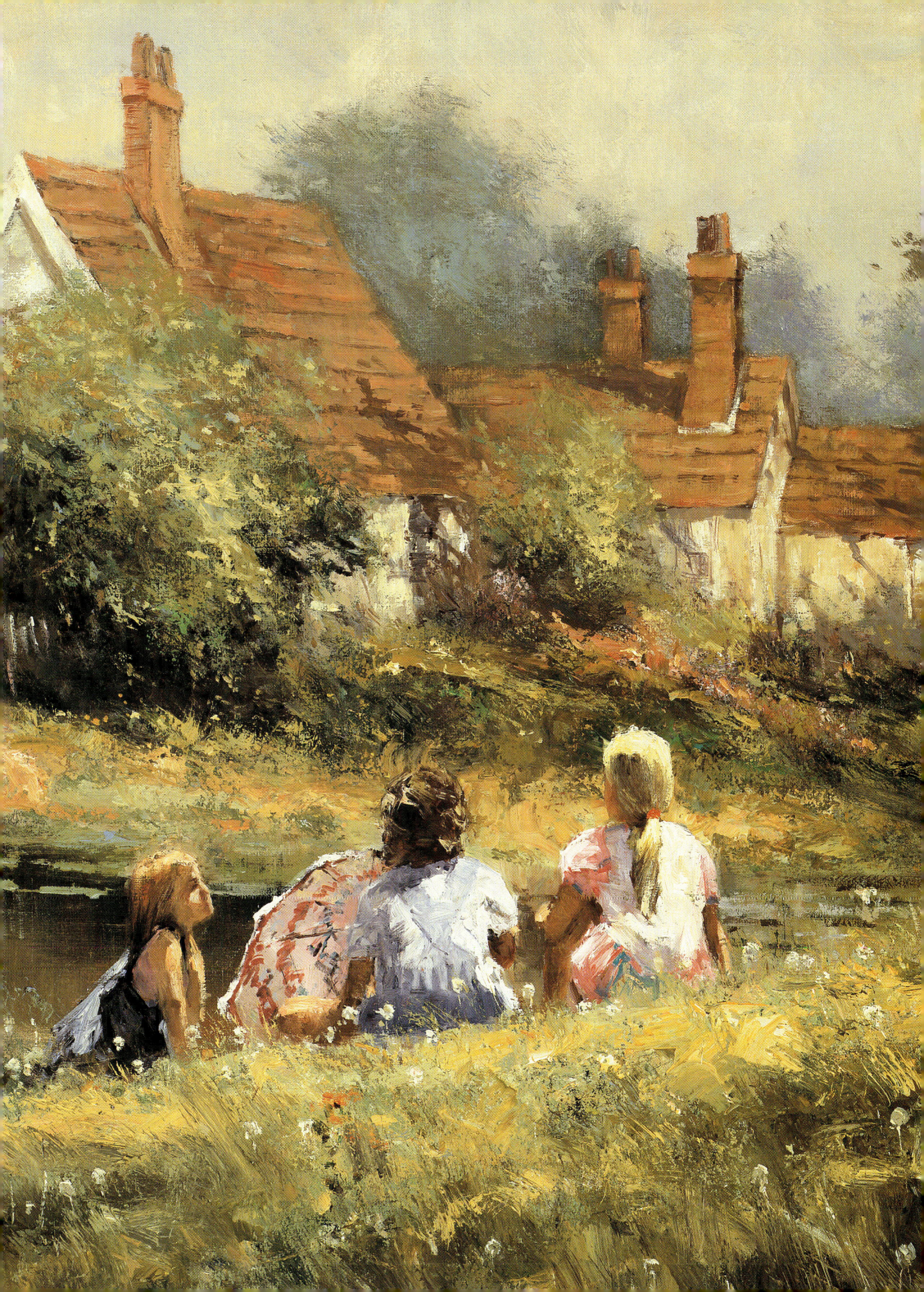

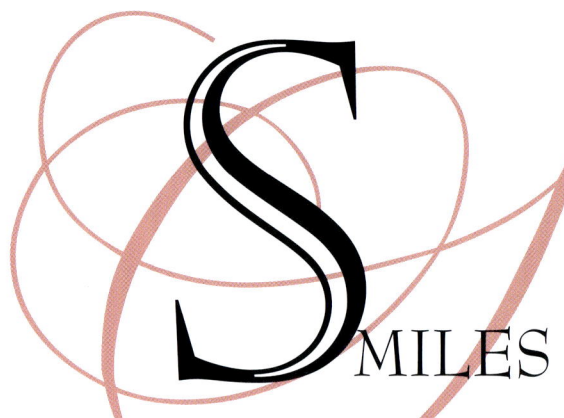

Smiles

The most memorable lesson
You can learn from a child
Is not what they say ... it is more
What they do with their smiles.
— Janice Somera

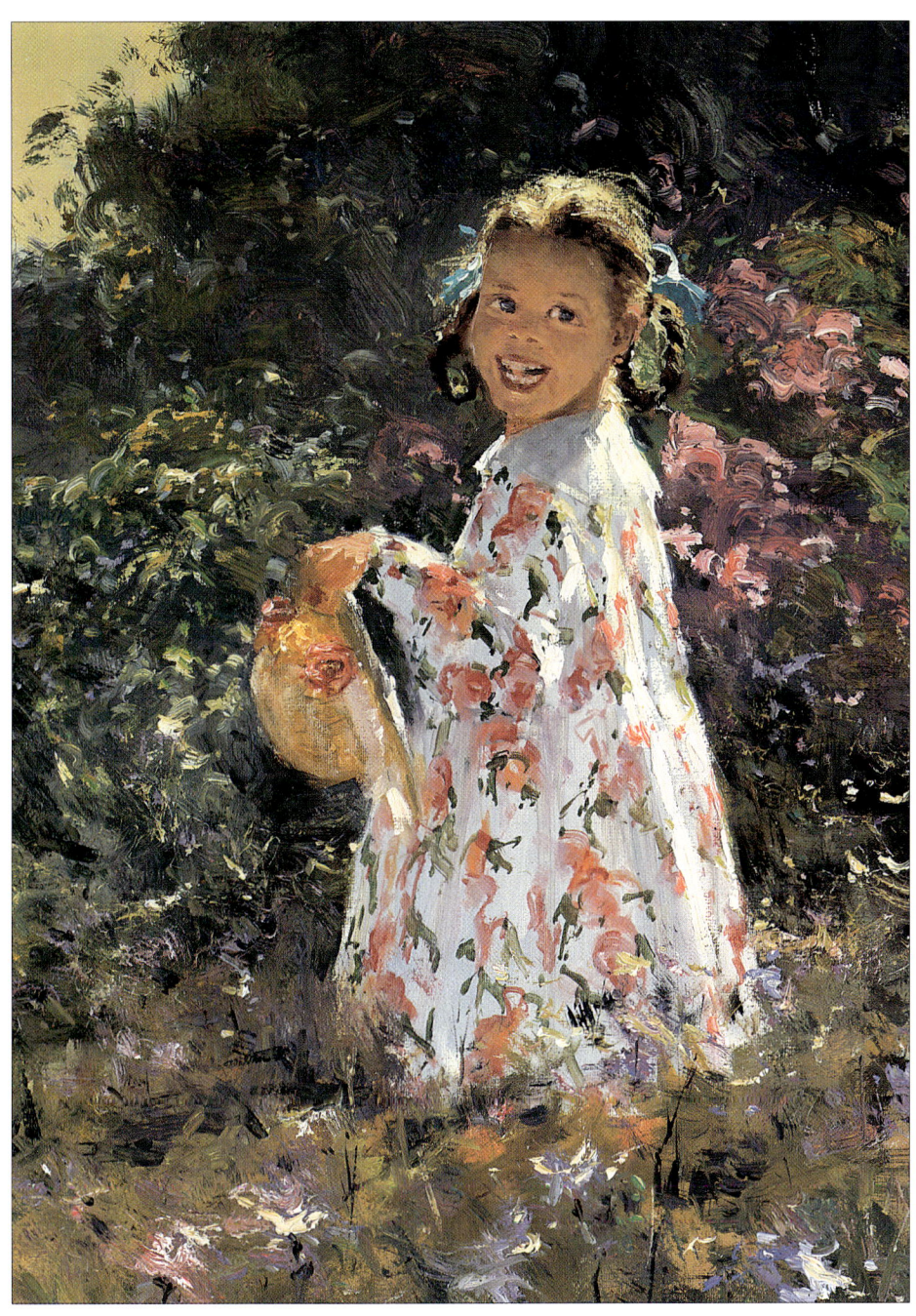

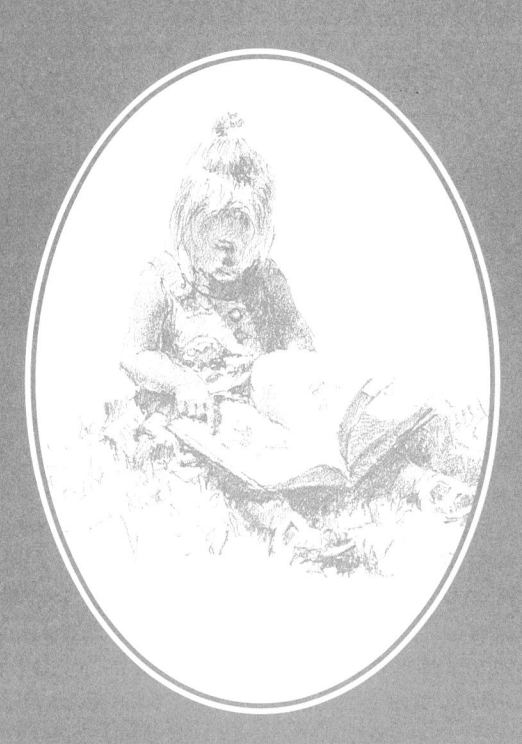